HOW TO
RAISE
A CHILD
YOU CAN
LIVE WITH

HOW TO
RAISE
A CHILD
YOU CAN
LIVE WITH

Clifford Stunden

WORD BOOKS
PUBLISHER
WACO, TEXAS

A DIVISION OF
WORD, INCORPORATED

How to Raise a Child You Can Live With

Scripture quotations in this publication are from the Revised Standard Version of the Bible (rsv), copyrighted 1946, 1952, © 1971, 1973 by the Division of Christian Education of the National Council of the Churches of Christ in the U.S.A., and are used by permission.
Scripture quotations marked niv are from the New International Version of the Bible, copyright © 1978 by the New York International Bible Society. Used by permission of Zondervan Bible Publishers.
Scripture quotations marked kjv are from the King James version of the Bible.

Library of Congress Cataloging-in-Publication Data

Stunden, Clifford, 1950–
    How to raise a child you can live with.

    1. Child rearing.   I. Title.
HQ772.S793 1986   649'.1   86–24535
ISBN 0–8499–0552–4

Printed in the United States of America

67898   BKC   987654321

*This book is dedicated
to the loving memory of*

FRANK CLIFFORD STUNDEN

*without whose life this book
would not have been possible.*

CONTENTS

ACKNOWLEDGMENTS

I want to thank the staff, elders, and friends of the West Covina Church of Christ, and Dr. James Dobson and my colleagues at Focus on the Family for their continued support and encouragement.

I'd like to give credit to Barbara and Alicia, whose expertise provided the finishing touch behind this book.

I also want to acknowledge Chuck and Diana, my good friends who faithfully prayed for me and whose mountain cabin provided the retreat I needed.

Most of all, my loving gratitude to my wife Diane and my two daughters Nicole and Laura, whose patience was tested beyond measure, and whose love and encouragement continually renewed my spirit.

1

The
Tragedy

HIS EYES WERE BLUE, his hair was brown, and he was the apple of his mother's and father's eye. His day had begun like most others under the warmth of an August sun in Southern California. It was especially enjoyable for his family because they were finally together again. The grief and separation of World War II had past, and it was time for the family to experience the joy of his presence and to dream the dreams that had been so rudely interrupted. It was time for him to play in the garden, to chase puppy dogs, and to run through the sprinklers as fast as his chubby little legs would carry him. He was nineteen months of toddling energy, and he was the joy of his family.

Like most toddlers, he was a flurry of activity. And as debris follows in the wake of a storm, so also his parents knew just where he had been. His spirit was unrelenting, and he had enough energy for both his mother and father. As was his custom most weekday mornings, he took a

Cook's tour of the household. Curiosity was the slogan for the day with special attention given to the "tookie man," the bakery truck driver, who made his weekly deliveries. Daddy and Granddad were off somewhere, but he had Mom and Nanny's full attention. It was going to be a great day.

There was a unique aura about this child, especially to his grandparents. Their long pilgrimage aboard the Majestic from England in 1935 and their immigration into a country barely a century and a half old was difficult for them to handle, as it would have been for any young couple. They experienced a full measure of hardship in their early years in America, but the birth of a third generation now in full swing gave them the assurance that the family name would continue, and made the adversity worth it all. Their loss of an entire dairy herd to hoof-and-mouth disease and the subsequent financial disaster suddenly didn't matter anymore. This child was their beloved Frankie, a son's son, and the fulfillment of many dreams.

Most of the morning chores were at their peak when the swirl of activity came to a standstill. What the wobbly-legged toddler had existed for all morning had finally arrived—the bakery truck, with its familiar whistle announcing its weekly delivery. His senses were filled with anticipation as the truck made its journey up the long driveway toward the house. The sheer thought of inspecting drawers full of pastries and "tookies" was more than his little mind could bear. There were sweet rolls and ice-cold milk—a literal bumper crop of the finest goodies known to children. So with great haste he led the parade with Mom and Nanny following him out the front door to this pantry on wheels. It was better than he had anticipated, with a potpourri of ginger snaps and chocolate chips at his disposal. After a small selection was made to accompany the morning tea, they retreated with some regret back into the house to enjoy the pickings for one more day.

A few minutes later his mother heard an odd noise coming from the front yard. "What was that sound?" She wondered aloud. Instantly, she questioned his whereabouts. But then she rested secure, for she thought him to be under the watchful eye of his grandmother. At the same moment, his grandmother believed that he was in the company of his mother. Unfortunately, the little lad had dropped one of his cookies on the ground as he returned to the house. He had hurriedly reached down to retrieve that dirty little cookie, which he prized so much, when the full weight of the truck and everything it was carrying rolled over his tiny frame.

What happened during the next few minutes would seem an eternity to his panic-stricken family. His mother rushed through the front door and down the porch steps to find the truck driver in shock, his face ashen white. With great distress he explained that it was an accident. He did not see her son in the rear-view mirror, nor did he hear his small voice. She seemed not to listen to him as she rushed to the side of her baby. He was lying under the truck with his motionless little legs extending to the side. As she reached down to raise his broken body into her arms, she recognized the inevitable signs of death in his precious blue eyes. She carried her baby through the kitchen into the livingroom and laid him gently down on the sofa. The young boy's father raced home from work, speeding through every signal and stop sign, hoping that he would arrive in time to help. The family physician was summoned immediately, but his training and experience would prove worthless in this case. Little Frankie's head was badly crushed, and not even a shot of adrenalin into his heart would preserve his life. Within full view of his mother and only a few short steps from the safety of his toys and teddybear, the child's life was swiftly swept away.

His mother and father fell weeping into one another's arms, and as they embraced beside his lifeless body, tears freely expressed the depth of their sorrow. As the day wore on, they attempted to console each other, but the familiar surroundings of the home only compounded the grief. Frankie's highchair was vacant. His bottle was empty. His favorite lullaby would go unsung. As his mother and father lay in bed that evening, they realized that the rustlings from his crib would no longer reassure them of his presence, and only silence would meet them in the morning.

In the aftermath of their son's death in August of 1949, only the sensitivity and caring by those closest to the family and the passage of time began to ease their pain. With this outpouring of love supporting them, the family knew it was in their best interest to leave the tragedy behind and restore their lives, but an unrelenting guilt locked them in place. What they understood in their minds was not what they were experiencing in their hearts. Guilt was in control. For this reason their emotions took on the dark, gloomy atmosphere of self-condemnation which pervaded the home.

The visitations to Frankie's grave began innocently enough, but due to the lingering guilt of the tragedy, his grandparents expected the whole family to make a weekly migration to his grave. With flowers picked only a few steps from where the tragedy occurred, the family proceeded there each Sunday for almost two years. It became a mandatory ritual. Although the parents wanted to release the grief, the grandparents' obsession with death would not permit them to be free of it. Sunday after Sunday, on Easter, on Frankie's birthday, and on the anniversary of his death the visitations continued. The cold, hard marble floors of the mausoleum echoed with the footsteps of the family as they proceeded down the long corridor toward the children's area and his crypt. At times his mother would stand at eye level to her son's crypt, pleading to hear just the whisper of a cry from within. She knew it would never come.

The lingering pain and grief were incalculable. The family doctor, fearing the possibility of suicide, warned that medication should be secured safely away from the boy's parents, especially his father. This environment of perpetual crises lasted for more than six months and caused close friends to fear for the family's future. Though the weekly visitations gradually became less frequent, the family continued to visit the grave every month for five more years. It wasn't until 1956, virtually seven years from the date of his death, that the monthly treks to the mausoleum ended.

This story which you have just read has been an emotional one for me to share because it is the true story of my own family. After the death of my brother Frankie, few events could have pulled my parents and family together like the birth of another child. And there was no doubt, especially in the eyes of my grandparents, that only another boy could replace the one they had lost. Responsibility for the death of my brother was carried primarily on the shoulders of my grandparents, who blamed themselves for what they believed to be unforgivable carelessness. Although Frankie's death was obviously an accident, the stubborn fact remained that my brother died while under their supervision and in their own front yard. Whether their thinking was rational or not, this fact grieved them all the more. Only another grandson could relieve their pain. And so month after month my family anticipated *the* announcement. The joyful words finally came six months after the tragedy. Nine months later their waiting ended. I was that new baby boy, the infant brother of their lost son.

When my birth was announced, Granddad wept openly on my father's shoulder. The composed mannerism of this Englishman was shaken. With my birth came a chance to undo the past. He would not make any further mistakes. And before my pink body was ever weighed on the hospital scale, the seeds of overprotection were being sown.

Though most children remember little of their early childhood years, I recall with clarity the overprotective environment into which I was born. With my brother's death still fresh in the minds of my family, they even cloned my name from my brother. He was christened Frank Clifford Stunden; I was named Clifford Frank Stunden, virtually guaranteeing that his death would be forever remembered through me. With this beginning, it was evident that I was viewed with a very special distinction. Hugged, cradled, and rocked by the hour, I was smothered with affection. It was surprising that I ever learned to walk since I was carried everywhere! Despite the genuineness of my grandparents' love, their desire to please made me understand at a very early age the art of obtaining my way with them. Like a thoroughbred race horse whose environment is monitored and controlled to sustain its every need, whatever I wanted my grandparents provided.

Throughout my preschool years, weekends were of particular delight because my grandparents would attend to my every beck and call. Resembling a twentieth-century King Tut with feet propped upon a footrest and a pillow for my head, I would place my orders for food and drink and without delay a banquet was cheerfully served. No use getting up—the cafeteria was brought to me. All the fried chicken that could be prepared was at my disposal. As my cup of tea would grow cold or empty, the rap of my spoon against its side would echo throughout their home only to bring the swift reply of more to drink. It has been said that some people are born with a silver spoon in their mouths; I was born with a silver bell in my hand.

With the halo my grandparents placed over my head, I could do no wrong. This however, was not the case with both of my sisters. There was a clear distinction between us pertaining to the manner in which love and discipline were communicated. Although my parents strongly objected to the warped sense of love and lack of discipline apportioned to me, they felt they had to comply in order to keep peace in the family. Days of bitter silence by my grandparents would result when my mother and father attempted to correct me in their presence. This silent treatment reflected my grandparents' true inability to cope emotionally with the chastening of their grandson, which they perceived as painful to me. In the aftermath of Frankie's death, they withdrew their hand of punishment. They could not permit themselves to intentionally inflict pain upon me. So with "slaves and servants" at my feet, I was in control.

On the one hand my parents wanted to discipline me,

but on the other my grandparents wanted to rescue me from that pain. The very grandson who was to restore joy into the family was a source of consternation. I was thirty pounds of preschooler pitting grandparents against parents in a vain struggle to see who was in control. Those who were close observers would see the winner clearly. As a result, there was a well-worn path through the neighbors' backyards from our house to my grandparents' house just a few doors away. It gave evidence to my desire to escape from the responsibilities of home in order to seek my selfish needs.

Even though everyone around me could see the consequences of my family's overprotective manner, I grew up with a distorted perception of my upbringing. Like most children, I cherished my relationship with my grandfather. I believed in him. When he spoke, his words were truth to me. Therefore, when he would fail to punish me, I would perceive from this that my behavior was proper. Neither could he permit himself to openly disagree with me, so as a result, I assumed that my thinking was correct. Based upon his unwillingness to discipline me, I concluded that I was always right and that I could do no wrong.

This belief system was illustrated very early in life during my first semester in kindergarten at the age of five. I tried to convince the entire class that the large tree in bloom on the school grounds was, in fact, a "boysenberry tree." Although my teacher attempted to correct me on this point, I objected because I was accustomed to having things my own way. Weeks of ridicule and teasing by the other children ensued because of my persistence, but this did not deter my stubborn self-assurance. With great anticipation my classmates and I waited for the "boysenberries" to fall off. I soon had to admit that walnuts make very poor jam! My bullheaded disposition was a reflection of the lack of discipline in my early childhood years which, when coupled with my foolish conviction that the world revolved around me, provided the basic ingredients for my stubborn nature.

No matter what the circumstances, my sole objective in

life centered around what would make me feel good, even at the expense of the interests or feelings of others. And a social gathering with my family was the perfect occasion for me to express my self-serving nature. A typical summer day in the valleys of Southern California consists of heat, usually beyond the century mark, and what the weather forecasters describe as "haze" (which all the natives truly know is smog.) Add humidity, dust, and an absence of shade, and you have all the ingredients for what some describe as the "crock-pot" days of summer. Throw a birthday party and a few grade school children into this environment and you set the stage for mayhem. This was a particularly frustrating event for me due to the fact that the birthday was not my own, and that most of the attention had been diverted from me to my younger cousin, who was the honored guest. Since I was not familiar with being out of the limelight, the best method to draw attention to myself was to instigate some mischief. Given the steamy weather, a garden hose was in order. I figured that cool water was the perfect remedy to beat the heat, so I proceeded to soak my skinny little body to my heart's delight. This activity was so refreshing that I decided to share my fortune with the rest of the crowd. However, the short stubby hose I was using wouldn't reach, so I extended its range through the use of a spray nozzle my grandfather used to wash off the kitchen porch. With the spigot fully turned on, a perfect, thirty-foot arch of spray caught my oldest cousin flush on the nose. Though his appearance resembled that of a soggy Cocker Spaniel, he was not amused. Instantly, a wave of fear overcame me and I dropped the hose as if to absolve myself of any responsibility—but it was too late. The culprit was obvious. The words he spoke to me at that moment have never been forgotten. As I stood before him with my head bent backward in order to see the top of his six-foot frame, he stated, *"You are a brat!"* His words reflected for the first time any confrontation in regard to my selfish nature. Despite my obvious culpability, my grandfather stepped in immediately and dismissed my carelessness toward my cousin as normal, childish fun. Therefore, because my grandfather exonerated me of any responsibility, I avoided discipline and failed to learn from my disobedience.

Because life was handed to me on a silver platter and I was sheltered from any form of responsibility, I concluded that other people were fully accountable to meet my needs. With this false assumption, I believed it to be the duty of others to get my work done. Instead of walking around the corner to school like the other children, I was driven by my grandfather. Instead of being encouraged to complete my homework and contend with the basics of the "three Rs," I simply asked my grandfather for the answers, which he readily provided. When fights and disagreements would take place between me and other children, he would always step in on my behalf.

Being rescued from responsibility and the normal everyday chores of life became a daily occurrence—a habit too hard to break. With this at the core of my spoiled nature, it became evident that my total reliance upon others to get my work done was permitting me to become incapable of meeting the challenges of life. The joy of being overprotected had failed to bring happiness . . . *I was miserable!*

Since my grandfather fought most of my battles for me throughout my childhood, his death when I was fourteen brought with it an overwhelming sense of desperation. My identity and worth had revolved around him instead of an accurate understanding of myself. With him gone, insecurity prevailed. My total dependence upon him to pave an easy road of life could no longer be maintained. Who was going to absorb the consequences of my irresponsibility? How was I to get good grades without him? In his absence, I developed an expertise in cheating on tests and homework to meet the demands of school, but this would only postpone the inevitable feelings of incompetence and insecurity. The overprotective and sheltered environment which I loved so much as a child and that catered to my every need was proving to be my curse. Plagued with inferiority and ill-equipped to socialize with my peers, I began to withdraw into myself, developing a shell that few would be able to penetrate. Faced with an uphill climb over that mountain called adolescence and a 1.6 grade point average at the beginning of high school, the pattern of retreat was set in motion. With my home as the proper setting, I created my own inner world of isolation.

Few explanations for my seclusion would prove socially acceptable, so becoming an electronics wizard furnished the perfect alibi. Radio parts, wires, transistors, and tubes would arrive at my home on a regular basis. Organized in a seemingly hopeless array of packages and boxes, the maze of apparent junk would begin to take shape. Armed with a soldering gun in one hand and a diagram in another, I gave total dedication to the project. After weeks of devotion, even to the point of skipping meals, the switch was turned on, and to my surprise, the radios would work.

To some it may have appeared that my hobby was a sign of genius, or that my isolation was a manipulative attempt to gain sympathy. But neither an intelligence quotient nor the exploitation of others was at issue here. Sixteen hours a day of hiding away from people should have been a clue as to the heart of the problem. No fancy explanations would be required in order to get to the root of it all. Intense fear of people would be answer enough—fear of letting them know who I really was—fear of attempting anything new—fear of failure and knowing that whatever self-respect I had left would be at risk. As I would lie awake in bed late into the night, tears betrayed my fear of growing up and finding myself alone. Most of all, I was terrified of being rejected.

With this powerful emotion of fear at the helm, the hours of isolation became pleasant compared to the world of reality. As a result of being controlled by my fear, withdrawal became the hallmark of my young adult life. The risk of incurring the rejection of others was not worth the potential of being accepted. I had become a social recluse in the truest sense of the term—but what a price I paid as a result. All of my adolescence was wasted by withdrawing from people, yet I continued to operate under the false assumption that somehow I would eventually grow up to feel secure.

If the decision had been left up to me, I would have chosen to separate myself from others for the rest of my life; however, certain events began to pry me away from my world of seclusion. After graduation from high school in 1968 at the peak of the Vietnam war, I was faced with the terrifying prospect of registering for the draft. The choice of my destiny was clear to me. I could either risk going to Vietnam or enlist in a branch of service that would permit me to stay out of combat. Although I may have been withdrawn, I wasn't naïve. Thus, I applied to enlist in the air force. At the moment I received my notification to appear, I was forced to recognize just how isolated I had become. I would speak only when spoken to, and walk with my eyes fixed to the ground, my posture resembling the curve of a banana. Nevertheless, I reported to the air force base and entered the headquarters building to commence the necessary paperwork and testing. As the sergeant called my name, a wave of nervousness made it necessary for me to visit, as my late grandfather would say, "the water closet." After asking directions I walked, as usual, with head bowed, to my destination. Everything seemed to be proceeding nicely until I began to hear the faint sound of high heels in the distance, and noticed that everyone who had entered the latrine after me was wearing women's shoes! The reality that I was trapped in the ladies' restroom was a moving experience—one that only the insane could truly comprehend. My first thought, of course, was to conceal my presence. Because my size twelve shoes were an instant giveaway, I lifted them off the floor; however, sitting on the throne with my feet raised to the sky was not going to solve the dilemma. As I sat in the stall surrounded by unsuspecting females, I contemplated my fate in the brig. How could I convince the military that I was not a voyeur or a sex maniac? Furthermore, how was I to explain to all my friends and relatives that I had become the first serviceman in history to be dishonorably discharged before taking the oath of allegiance? These thoughts brought me little relief and failed to answer the fundamental question: How was I to extricate myself without being noticed? Bolting out of the stall like a wild horse would only draw attention to myself; so there I sat in a catatonic state, hoping for an opportune moment to escape. Fortunately, I was eventually able to flee undetected, and was accepted into the reserves without receiving a "Section 8."

Although this experience taught me to walk with my head up, it failed to conquer the source of my isolation from others. Many favorable opportunities were made available to me to enhance my social skills, but I was too afraid to take advantage of those occasions. On a rather humid afternoon in July after working all day at the air force base, the only thought in my mind was to return home as quickly as my Volkswagen bug could do so. Soaking my body in a pool on a hot day in L.A. while sipping a glass of iced tea was utmost on my priority list. To my surprise, upon returning home, forty college students from my sister's church had invaded my backyard and overtaken everything but the television set. Few of these folks knew who I was, and based upon my antisocial behavior, their initial impression of me must have been one of uncertainty. Dressed in my long-sleeved, khaki fatigue uniform, I retired alone to the den. With shades pulled and blinds drawn, the remaining hours of the afternoon were spent perspiring in a non-air-conditioned room while watching arm wrestling on the "Wide World of Sports." Though invited to join the poolside festivities, I could only muster enough courage to crack open the blinds every hour or so to take a look outside. Peering through the window, I could catch a glimpse of the kind of relationships I had always longed for. The years in service for my country afforded me many of these opportunities, but as usual, the fear of rejection continued to maintain its grip on me.

Emotional pain is a tremendous motivator, and as I approached the pit of loneliness, I reached out to others in desperation. Perhaps someone would reciprocate in friendship. After receiving an invitation from the minister of my sister's church, I spent an entire weekend at a camp attended by many college people. To me, this act was a last resort. What a predicament I had placed myself in. Once the camp had convened, I was "trapped like a rat." On the one hand the college students were getting too close to me, which was enormously threatening, and yet at the same time I desired their attention. There was something odd about these young people. They seemed to think I had an intrinsic sense of worth. They didn't avoid me as others had in the past. Nevertheless, I was wary of their motives. What was in it for them? I remained extremely cautious of their intentions throughout the weekend; however, as it progressed I began to realize that Jesus Christ was the key to their motivation and love. Before the retreat was over, I committed my life to serving Him.

When I asked God to become Lord of my life, I came to understand that conquering the summit of my insecurities would not be accomplished through withdrawing from others. I had followed the blueprint of my own design, convinced all along that it would produce the fruit of self-acceptance and the respect of others. Yet it did not. My method of coping with life's demands had not brought me the joy and happiness that I had long sought. Only the Lord could provide the power and the people for my new identity.

Very few of my friends today remember that tall, skinny kid in 1971. Those who do can attest to the fact that the person who left for that college retreat was not the same man who returned. On September 12, the final evening of camp, I returned to the church I had rarely attended, and testified to the transformation that had occurred. With the

Sunday evening service drawing to a close, I stepped forward, in the custom of the church, to formally dedicate my life to Christ. Within full view of over two hundred people, I stood before strangers and spoke with a new-found eloquence far removed from my normal self. To many who were present I must have appeared like so many others who had become invigorated at a church camp. Yet, for those who had known me throughout my life, my countenance at that moment must have sparked disbelief. Was this the same person with whom they had been raised?

As a young, fledgling Christian, I was told that God looked upon me as a new creation. Though I believed in what He said, doubts still crept in. Withdrawing from others over the years had left me with scars that continued to haunt me, especially my inability to communicate. Despite overcoming my unwillingness to socialize, I was pressed from every side to express myself. This was most difficult for me with women. I could not figure out how to converse with them. I had dated only twice throughout my entire adolescence, and those opportunities were set up by my sister. This lack of experience robbed me of the confidence I needed to talk. I simply had nothing to say.

As a member of my church's college class, a long list of social opportunities awaited me. With a substantial amount of prodding I reluctantly agreed to attend an upcoming party. Just because I had decided to go didn't mean I was lying awake at night in anxious anticipation of this event. So with procrastination as my plan, I sat in my car that evening hoping that I would go unnoticed. To my surprise, a young college student named Diane refused to accept my withdrawal. She recognized me as the one who spoke so boldly at church just a few weeks before. That social gathering started a relationship that continues to this day. Because of my low self-esteem, I vacillated in my early commitments toward her, but her love for me steadily grew. It took three years after our wedding for me to become fully convinced that my wife would not leave me, that I was worthy of her devotion. Eventually, her love played a critical role in helping me overcome my deep sense of inadequacy.

The consequences of overprotection and my feeble attempts to cope with it became clear to me after Christ came into my life. With His love, the love of untold others, and especially my wife Diane's love, we were able to transform my life from its overprotective past. Tremendous barriers did have to be overcome in order to accomplish this miracle. Chief among these was my inability to socialize with people. Though it is still very difficult for me to believe, my wife swears to this day that when she first met me I was incapable of holding a meaningful conversation with anyone. It has been jokingly said that some people cannot walk and chew gum at the same time. In my case I literally could not speak and look someone in the eye at the same time. I was once blind to my lack of social skill, the complete absence of self worth, and my inability to express warmth and love. With God's grace I have faced these obstacles squarely and have overcome the consequences of an overprotective and spoiled childhood.

The threads of overprotection are sown early into the framework of a child, and for this reason it is vital that parents understand the potential for doing so occurs as early as the first few months of life and beyond. The roadsigns that lead us to identify the overprotective parent are unclear to some. Because of this, if we are to avoid the consequences of such parenting techniques we must ultimately confront our own emotional nature, the styles of parenting that we have grown accustomed to, and subtle influences that the world imposes upon us to undermine our Judeo-Christian values. The pressures that encumber us as parents to raise our children in this society can be enormous. Since our little ones cannot raise themselves, it is vital that we equip them with the best possible tools to confront the challenges of this world. If we fail to do so, we will be faced with the dim prospect of self-centered, spoiled children, who grow up to be self-centered, spoiled adults instead of the successes we have always dreamed about. It is in regard to this issue that I have been brought to this occasion of writing the book, *How to Raise a Child You Can Live With.*

2

The Surrendered Household

GOOD, LOVING PARENTS can overprotect their children, and it is those of us who truly care about their welfare that are the most vulnerable. From the earliest moments of life we want the best for our child. Before his tiny lungs become fully inflated and he rests his wobbly little head upon his mother's breast, his parents have contemplated how they can fully meet his needs. He is completely dependent upon them, and his desires and wants are of utmost importance to his folks. Prior to his birth they have exercised painstaking care to assure that the nursery walls are painted, the crib is constructed, and a reservation secured for a Cabbage Patch doll. Late into the evenings, Mom and Dad have tread on the brink of divorce discussing for the fiftieth time what they are going to name their newborn child. And for what reason? Because his parents love him and want to give him the very best. We do this justifiably and with great enthusiasm because our children are the joy of our lives.

While we are concerned about loving and providing for the needs of our children, we are confronted with another great issue in regard to their upbringing. Because of the natural love we have for them we assume a great risk—the risk allowing our love to become misguided in the form of overprotection or permissiveness. With this as a possibility, we make every effort to teach our children through loving discipline so that they will grow up into secure, caring, responsible adults. Last on our agenda is to raise an unruly child. Therefore, with a watchful eye, we become keenly aware of their mannerisms and how they are perceived by relatives, the person in the grocery check-out line, and the parents of the child next door. We pray that God will spare us from that tap on the shoulder while we are in worship service, informing us that our son or daughter is acting rebelliously in Bible school class.

A few years ago my wife and I were invited to one of the finest weddings we've ever attended. The families of the bride and groom had taken great care to decorate the church, choose the right flowers, and plan a very nice reception dinner. After everyone had been seated, the ushers escorted the bridesmaids to the altar of the church in the traditional custom. The ring bearer and flower girl stunned all the guests with their miniature tuxedo and dress, and the bride made her appearance at the head of the aisle to be received by her anxious groom. Everyone was in place, and everything was in order. Five minutes into the ceremony the ring bearer began to twitch and squirm. With his parents in obvious distress, they attempted to graciously control their son's behavior by whispering commands from the front row; however, he paid no attention. His actions quickly degenerated from fidgeting in mild discomfort to hopping up and down like a frog and sprinting to and fro across the front of the sanctuary. Finally, in desperation, the father grabbed his son's arm, but before he could escort him out the side door, the four year old yelled out an obscenity— a word that might be used to describe steer manure! The minister did his best to continue as if nothing had occurred, but the obvious could not be ignored. The ceremony was disrupted, and Mom and Dad were utterly embarrassed, feeling like failures.

As parents we are caught in a dilemma. On the one hand we want to give our children all the joys and comforts of life. We want their lives to be better than our own. Yet at the same time we don't want to give them so much that they fail to understand the value of it all—becoming ungrateful and disobedient, expecting others to give them a free ride in life.

We all have certain assumptions as to who the overprotected child might be. Some of us have concluded that it is the "only child" who falls into this category. Maybe it is the child whose mother is afraid to allow him to play in sports for fear of him being injured. A majority might say that parents who are reluctant to have their young children watched by a babysitter or spend the night at a friend's home fall victim to this style of parenting. Others are convinced that a sheltered environment is guaranteed for the boy or girl whose family may have suffered a tragedy such as my own. Some of these may be legitimate expressions of overprotection, but if we allow these examples to restrict our view then we will not only stereotype many an undeserving parent, but we will stop short in our understanding of that which lies at the heart of the matter. To fully comprehend this issue and its implications upon us as parents, we must expand our definition of overprotection in order to recognize the distinction between it and discipline.

Discipline lovingly teaches and equips our children with the spiritual, emotional, and physical tools necessary for them to conquer the trials and demands of life, and holds them accountable when they rebel against pre-established guidelines. Overprotection, which has love at its core, short-circuits the disciplinary process. In our ambition to be a good parent, we may unknowingly overrespond to the needs of our children by surrendering to their selfish wishes and desires. Though well-meaning, this attempt at discipline prevents our children from being held accountable for their actions, culminating in a low self-esteem and rebelliousness. This is brought about in several ways.

The Wall of Protection

As any caring parent would, we desire to shield our children from danger. We baby-proof certain rooms of the house, place caustic liquids and detergents out of reach, and cover up electrical outlets with plastic plugs. From the moment they are capable of coordinating their tiny hands to their mouths, we are on guard to prevent them from doing everything from swallowing a dead centipede to committing the most serious of injuries.

Once when our daughter Nicole was barely two years old, she became intrigued with the steam billowing upwards from the hot tea I had placed on the living room table. It was not uncommon for her to sneak past Mom and Dad to play outside in the dog's water, so she must have thought my cup of tea to be a miniature version. She was not aware, however, that this liquid had just been zapped in the microwave. To her, it was just another in a long list of fascinating playthings. But to me as her father, it represented the perfect opportunity for serious injury. As I began to move the tea to a more secure location, Nicky attempted to submerge her fingers in the scalding liquid. Fortunately, I was able to step in and grab her hand, but at the same time while I had her left hand suspended in mid-air, she plunged her right hand into the hot tea. Though she was quick to remove it, her tears expressed the extent of her mistake. To my relief, she experienced no permanent injury and I was able to explain the circumstances to my wife so that I saved my marriage from extinction. Though my daughter's mishap was a regrettable accident, most parents will exercise great care to guard their children from this type of injury, and it would be foolish to suggest that protecting them from imminent harm constitutes a case for overprotection.

The key to avoid overprotecting a child, however, lies in how we as parents react to those trials of life that jeopardize their spiritual and emotional health. As the sin and stress of this world confront our sons and daughters, we are faced with the most difficult decision we will ever have to make. Shall we allow them to experience the harsh realities of life, praying that we have adequately prepared them to do so, or do we step in to prevent them from going through that pain? To choose the former requires a great deal of courage and self-confidence on our part. We, as parents, must affirm our trust in God in spite of the painful circumstances that our children are going through, knowing that He will reward our efforts if we prepare them to meet those trials of life. We do this because we want to insure them a happy future. Therefore, if we are to prevent ourselves from building a wall of protection around our kids we must learn to override or set aside our natural parental instinct to rescue them from pain and suffering.

A few weeks after our daughter's first birthday we were awakened at 3:00 A.M. by her continual screaming. After being jolted out of bed, we found her with a high fever and in great pain. Though we attempted to comfort her, she would not be consoled, and we spent the remainder of our sleepless night worrying as to what the problem might be. When morning arrived, we were finally able to see her pediatrician, and to our surprise we were told that she had a rather common type of ear infection—easily controlled by antibiotics.

It appeared that as soon as she recovered from one of these infections it would be followed by another only a few weeks later. This struggle lasted for over a year! Despite the obvious expense of the prescriptions and visiting the doctor twice a month, we were informed that Nicole was risking permanent hearing loss if her infections failed to stop. After numerous appointments with different physicians, we were asked to give permission for her to undergo an operation to place "tubes" in her ears. We knew it was a relatively simple procedure, but this knowledge failed to alleviate our anxiety. Despite our misgivings, we decided that for Nicky's welfare we had to proceed.

The day of the hospital visit arrived and, after she was admitted, Nicky was placed in a child's bed with a plexiglass cage to prevent her from climbing out. Once her pre-operation shot was administered, we knew it would only be a few minutes before the nurses took her away. Logic said that we were doing the right thing. However, our hearts ached as we saw our daughter in what she perceived to be a threatening, uncomfortable environment—longing for the security of her mother and father. Through tears of our own, we witnessed that sense of abandonment in her eyes as they wheeled her down the long corridor toward surgery. At this moment, we could have yielded to her discomfort, picked her up, and taken her to the security of her home. But we did not. Though we knew she was in emotional pain, we had to set aside our own emotions momentarily for the good of her long-term health. For her sake, we could not rescue her.

Occasionally, we can overrespond in our desire to protect our children from spiritual and emotional harm. As a result, we place a wall of protection between them and pain. In our honest attempt to shield them from unpleasantness, we inadvertently sweep away one of the most profound truths of life—the reality that this world can be painful and unfair. This is a sobering thought, and it would be much easier for us to ignore this fact. Therefore, if we erect such a barrier, we take the risk of leading our children to believe that someone will always run to their aid, delivering them from their trials and failures.

This is a very sensitive issue. I do not want to imply that we should make life as tough as possible for our kids so that in our attempt to help them take responsibility for their actions they, in turn, become hardened and insensitive themselves. Rather, our attention should be focused on the dependent relationship that exists between parent and child which develops from the moment of birth.

Parents of a newborn, especially the mother, will testify that a bond is created between them and their infant child, from the womb to birth and beyond, a closeness that is nurtured and strengthened as the child gets older. This is a naturally healthy process which guarantees the provision of not only the child's physical needs but his emotional requirements as well. This bond is very strong and is difficult to give up. However, in order for our children to progress in their growth toward maturity, we must gradually relinquish a portion of the closeness. Throughout the course of our children's lives we are involved in a continual process of equipping them with the spiritual, emotional, and physical tools required to prepare them for adulthood. As we assume the heavy burden, we must not only communicate these values verbally, but we must slowly hand over the responsibility for them as well. In time, we will begin to transform their dependency upon us to themselves and God, which is critical for their long-term character development. If, as a child grows older, he fails in his emancipation from his parents, an overwhelming sense of inadequacy will develop which impairs him from making mature decisions on his own. He will never believe in himself, which will culminate in a low self-esteem. The wall of protection, which was designed to shelter him from harm, has now handicapped him from being fully equipped to confront life and its painful circumstances.

Childish Manipulation

"He is my helper. He is my helper. He is my helper." These were the lyrics to a song my daughter was singing as she returned home from church one Sunday morning. Her tune intrigued me because I had never heard it before, so I inquired further. "Nicole, who is your helper?" "Jesus is my helper," she replied. I was so proud. At her tender age, she was already beginning to comprehend one of the roles that Christ assumed in her life. I wanted to probe the depth of her theological understanding even further, so I asked her, "Nicole, what does Jesus help you do?" Her reply: "Jesus helps me go to McDonald's!"

Parents in our culture have more information available to them about child rearing and discipline than any other generation in history. With a multitude of books, tapes, films, and seminars at our disposal, we still have great difficulty recognizing and accepting one critical area of our children's nature—their natural inclination to be selfish. I laughed when I heard my daughter's response to the question I had asked her because I found it to be funny and cute. Moments such as these are precious, and we look forward to them. However, after thinking further about her reply, I had to admit that, in reality, my daughter was a cute little sinner! Though she was yet to celebrate her third birthday, she was already twisting one of God's truths into something that would achieve her own purposes, and she was using her mother and father to accomplish that goal.

A number of years ago, a mother and her young daughter entered our counseling offices for what Mom called a "child discipline problem." Within the first session, she began to describe how Jenny[1] was rebellious and unmanageable—demanding her own way. The circumstances within the home had deteriorated to such a degree that its very atmosphere was being controlled by the mood of the girl with Mom having to knuckle-under to her every whim. Denise was a bright and intelligent woman who was well-read in her knowledge of parenting. Her disciplinary skills were basically good, and she prided herself in her ability to communicate love and esteem to her daughter. Still, something was wrong. During our next appointment, it became very clear to all of us that Jenny knew her mother very well. Before too long, her daughter communicated to us a list of ten ways she could force her mother to become angry and lose control! Jenny was five years old.

During her short tenure on this planet, Jenny had developed a keen awareness of her mother's disciplinary measures and tolerance limit, and how she could manipulate her way around them. Denise was shocked. How could one so young get to the point of dominating a full-grown adult? To answer this question by simply stating that her daughter just happened to be exceptionally bright would be a misunderstanding of Jenny's character. Jenny is selfish. She is not the exception in this regard; she is the norm. In the Old Testament, King Solomon explains in the Proverbs that, "Foolishness is bound in the heart of a child . . ."[2] Children, by nature, have captured within their hearts a propensity to be in control and to manipulate the environment for their selfish purposes. Though this is not always a conscious effort, it is innate within them. I hesitate, at this point, to describe our children with such strong language. I surely do not want to paint a diabolical picture of our kids, or to suggest that they are devoid of any goodness, because they exemplify God's character so many ways. My twelve-month-old daughter, Laura, was sitting in her highchair the other day awaiting her evening feeding. As I said, "Let's pray," Laura looked up at me, smiled, and put her hands together as did the rest of the family. I couldn't pay someone for the feelings of joy that overcame me at that moment. Laura was beginning to take possession of one of the godly principles that my wife and I had taught her, and it thrilled our hearts. Before our meal was over, however, Laura, because I wouldn't give her something she wanted, angrily threw a green bean at me, narrowly missing my nose. We can see from this that within just a few short minutes, my daughter exemplified two elements of her character—her willingness to express God's virtues, and her stubborn desire to please herself.

In order to avoid the possibility of overprotecting our children, we must not only refrain from building a wall of protection, but we must also accept the fact our sons and daughters are selfish by nature. If we can come to grips with their self-centeredness, we will begin to see how they can manipulate us into sheltering them. This is accomplished, primarily, through the use of three basic emotions.

Love

Every parent wants to avoid hearing those dreaded words, "I don't love *you.*" Most of us, however, have already heard this from our son or daughter, typically after we have disciplined them. These words are very powerful, and they will stop any parent in his tracks. If a child ever expresses doubt about his love for his mother or father, it will immediately invoke within his parents a reassessment of what *they* may have done wrong. Through the use of these words, children produce a startled look on Mom and Dad's face and hope that it will result in more lenient disciplinary measures. *A child learns very quickly that his threat of withdrawing love can persuade most adults to meet his selfish desires.*

I had mentioned earlier that when I was a youngster my grandfather treated me like a king. This sincere expression of his love began innocently enough when I was a baby. But as I grew older, I came to understand that I could use his love to my own advantage. My grandfather was a staunch Englishman who had a precise way of preparing his traditional "tea and toast." The tea was always brewed, and served with milk or cream. The toast was lightly buttered, cut down the middle (not diagonally). He wanted to please his grandson, so he served it to me as a way of showing me that I was important to him. I was fully capable of getting it myself, yet I learned that I could manipulate him into doing so by the use of a pouting face, dawdling, or the words, "I don't love you." It didn't matter whether or not I actually *said* the words, because through my body language I expressed how displeased I was with him if he didn't serve me. Soon, I had him trained to wait on me hand and foot. Though I was just four years old, I was able to exploit my grandfather's love by threatening him with the withdrawal of my own.

I surely do not want to suggest that we avoid being misused in this fashion by not responding to the needs of others. Christ calls us to adopt the attitude of a servant; however, children need to be trained to understand this principle because, by nature, they can use others selfishly. With this in mind, parents must recognize that a child can learn how to misapply God's law of love to serve his own desires.

Fear

Those of us who have taken a basic course in psychology will remember that fear is a function of what is called our "fight or flight mechanism." This is an element of our human physiology which works in conjunction with our brain to protect us in times of danger. When we, or someone that we love, are threatened by something harmful, we usually respond in one of two ways. We either run from it (flight) or we protect ourselves (fight). This mechanism is natural within all human beings, and when it is applied properly, it works in our best interest.

Imagine that you are traveling with your family on vacation and that you must stop at a railroad crossing for a slow-moving freight train. After what seems an eternity, the caboose finally passes in front of you, and the children wave "bye-bye" to the conductor and brakeman. As you begin to proceed on your way, you car stalls—right over the tracks! Suddenly, bells begin to ring, signals start flashing, and the crossing-gates drop before your eyes. As you look out the driver's window on your left, there appears in the distance the bright, penetrating light of another train heading your direction. At this moment, you don't conduct a family meeting to discuss all the options you have available. Naturally, your response is one of sheer panic with all of your attention focused on removing your family to safety. Thus, as we can see from this example, fear plays an important role in the preservation of our lives. There are moments, however, when the flight mechanism can cause us to shelter our children.

Children are very perceptive of our emotional state of mind, especially as it relates to this emotion. They learn from us that under the right conditions fear will motivate us to protect them. Though it can be a very difficult concept to believe, children are fully capable of utilizing this emotion to control their mother or father hoping that they can be protected from accepting responsibility. This principle was illustrated a few years ago with a young married couple who attended a church close to my own. Bob and Elaine had struggled throughout their lives with severe allergies, and they began to notice that their son had begun to suffer from these symptoms as well. Unfortunately, their five year old, Brian, developed complications. One evening in the spring of 1980, the father came to tuck his son into bed and found him gasping for air as if he was choking on a foreign object. Afraid for his son's life, Bob summoned Elaine to assist him in finding the source of the problem. As she approached Brian she could see that sense of desperation on his face as he struggled to breathe. Even though Elaine had some medical training, they were both helpless to stop him from coughing and wheezing. Without hesitation, they rushed him to the hospital a few blocks away. Upon entering the emergency room, it was obvious to the doctor that the young boy was in severe distress. With some explanation from the parents, it appeared that his current medical problem may have been related to his allergies. Upon further diagnosis, it was determined that Brian had suffered an acute asthma attack. After receiving an injection of medication, he recovered quickly, and he returned home that evening with his very relieved mother and father.

Over the course of the next year, Bob and Elaine returned their son to the emergency room three more times for exactly the same reason. Then to our surprise, those of us who were close to the family began to witness an interesting turn of events. It appeared that Brian's attacks were becoming more and more closely associated with the personal relationship he had with his father—especially as it related to matters of discipline and irresponsibility. Bob was the primary disciplinarian in the home and when his son would become rebellious or demanding he would lovingly correct him. For the most part, Brian was an obedient child, but for some reason which his parents could not explain, he was becoming increasingly unruly. As father and son confronted each other in this test of wills, Brian became anxious, sometimes developing a severe asthmatic condition which required emergency treatment. At this juncture, it is vital that we pause to make a very important observation. Every time Brian's asthma would flare up, his parents would immediately forget about his rebelliousness and their discipline of him. Obviously, this was a justifiable response since many times he required medication. However, let's look at the situation from Brian's point of view. He had observed over the past few months that his asthma struck fear in the hearts of his parents, culminating in an escape from the consequences of his misbehavior. Unknowingly, in their honest attempt to fight for their son's health, the parents had inadvertently withdrawn from holding him accountable for his rebelliousness. With this knowledge, it is easy to see how Brian could unconsciously use his medical condition to manipulate his parents into sheltering him, or possibly spoiling him, to meet his selfish desires.

At this moment, I run the greatest risk of appearing cold or insensitive towards those children who are struggling with physical pain. I surely would not want this to be the case. My heart goes out to Brian and all the other boys and girls who suffer from this or any other illness. And I would suggest to his mother and father that they continue to be extra sensitive toward their son, seeking swift medical attention when necessary. However, Brian still needs to pick up his toys, be respectful, and do his homework like any other child. It would not be in his best interest for his parents to allow him to become undisciplined as a result of his medical condition.

Fear plays an important role—to protect us in times of danger. However, children can learn to use fear to control those whom they love. If allowed to do so, they will soon believe that this emotion could become a license for being protected from accepting responsibility.

Anger

Not only can the emotions of love and fear serve as foundations for sheltering a child, but anger can do so as well. As is the case with both of my daughters, anger is the natural response of a child who is unable to get his own way. Whether it is expressed directly through a "temper tantrum" or with a subtle scowl, anger is often used by children to take leadership from those around them in order to get their own way.

This reminds me of Nancy, a woman I met at a "Child Discipline Seminar" which I conducted five years ago. She had three children—a three year old, an eighteen month old, and a newborn. She told me a story about the most dreaded event in her life—grocery shopping! For those of you who are not familiar with what an ordeal this can become, let me give you her example. Despite trying to maintain her sanity on the way to the store, Nancy had to cope with her three-foot-tall, fifty-pound preschooler, Andrea, who was the self-appointed "grocery cart puller." Of course, Nancy's goal was to get groceries; however, with her children in the first cart there wasn't enough room for the food, which meant she had to get another cart. With her infant daughter secured safely in her infant seat and nestled in the back of the cart, the toddler, Jamie, took her place in the front. Once this was organized, Andrea lead a four-part "train" down the aisle, first with herself, then the shopping cart half full of kids, then Mommy, and finally the empty cart. As they proceeded down the aisle, Andrea began to go back and forth picking cans indiscriminately off the shelves, dropping them over the top of the cart and down onto her little sister's toe. With Jamie screaming in pain, the baby, who had been napping, awoke crying. Mom, who was embarrassed because all the other customers were watching, reached down into the diaper bag to get a bottle in an attempt to quiet her newborn. Finally, it appeared that Nancy was beginning to bring order out of chaos. As she was attempting to discipline Andrea for playing with the cans, Andrea got very angry and raced off pulling the grocery cart, with her sisters going along for the ride. Leaving the rest of the food behind, Nancy sprinted in desperation after her three daughters hoping that she could prevent a multi-cart collision and severe injury. Once Mom caught up with them at the check-out line, Andrea, who knew she was really in trouble, flopped to the floor, kicking her chubby little legs in defiance. With such an angry child, is it any wonder that Nancy feels extreme pressure to avoid a scene, cave-in under Andrea's rebellion, and give her what she wants?

I doubt that Andrea planned this event; nevertheless, she ended up in control of the situation with her mother feeling guilty and embarrassed. When she goes to the store next time, Nancy will experience great temptation to acquiesce to her daughter's selfish desires. If Mom does so, Andrea will learn that under the right circumstances and within the proper environment, she can stimulate her mother to become incapacitated by her anger, and thereby protect herself from the consequences of her misbehavior.

We can run the risk of overprotecting our children as a direct result of our love for them. If we place a wall of protection around them, thereby sheltering them from the painful realities of this world, we will incapacitate them from responding to life's demands. When combined with their selfish nature, this enables them to be in control of their environment, with Mom, Dad, and the rest of the family living in partial surrender to their will.

I have found that after years of working with families

in counseling that those who overprotect their children do so through consistent behavioral patterns. As a result of my experience, I have listed below questions that relate to the most common reasons why family members build the wall of protection and yield to childish manipulation. They can be used as a guide in helping you to determine if these characteristics are demonstrated in your own life. Please check the appropriate column.

CHECKLIST OF OVERPROTECTION

	YES	NO
1. Do you find yourself loosening your standards of discipline in order to appease your child's wishes?	——	——
2. Is the primary source of your self-esteem derived from your children?	——	——
3. Have you suffered the loss of one of your children?	——	——
4. Do you pick up your child every time he cries, even though after checking on him you realize that there may not be any identifiable reason for his tears?	——	——
5. Has your spouse, a close relative, or a friend ever brought to your attention that the amount of time you spend with your children is having negative consequences upon your marriage?	——	——
6. When you were a child, did your parents use a rigid or authoritarian style of parenting?	——	——
7. Do you consistently allow your child to dictate your daily schedule?	——	——

8. Do you allow only those who are in your immediate family to care for your children?   ___ ___

9. Do you withhold your children from participating in sports or other physical activities for fear of them being injured?   ___ ___

10. When your child is faced with a distressing situation, either physical or emotional in nature, do you find yourself stepping in to fight his battles for him?   ___ ___

11. When your child is being disciplined by someone other than yourself, does he consistently run to you for a second opinion?   ___ ___

12. If you have more than one child, have others pointed out that you have a tendency to show favoritism toward one of them in particular?   ___ ___

13. Has one of your children suffered from a disability or a life-threatening illness?   ___ ___

14. Have you, on more than one occasion, paid off the indebtedness of one of your grown-up children?   ___ ___

15. When your child falls behind in or has difficulty understanding his homework, have you found yourself doing it for him?   ___ ___

16. Do you avoid discussing with your junior high or high school age child such issues as sexuality, alcohol, drugs, movies, rock videos, etc.?   ___ ___

17. Your child has become an adult and has chosen to move out of the home. But, like the Prodical Son, he has totally mismanaged his life. Have you on more than one occasion, allowed him to move back in with you even though he has refused to change his lifestyle?   ___ ___

18. Are you currently allowing your high

school age son or daughter to stay at home
even though he or she may be involved in
such a sinful lifestyle that it is tearing your
family apart?   ___   ___

19. Do you believe in the old adage that "boys
    will be boys"?   ___   ___

20. Are you currently separated or divorced?   ___   ___

As in my family, there may come a point in time when
you find yourself responding to your children in one of the
ways listed above. Individually, these examples should not
be used to prove that one is an overprotective parent. However, based upon my experience, most parents who are
overprotective exhibit a minimum of two. If you endorsed
four or more, then serious consideration should be given to
the negative consequences that may result regarding your
child and his long-term relationship with you.

---

[1] The names and places of those mentioned within the counseling illustra-
tions have been changed in order to protect their confidentiality.
[2] Proverbs 22:15

3

The Foundations
of Overprotection

MANY OF US KNOW at least one person whom we believe to be an overprotective parent. We scratch our heads in dismay wondering how it is that they fail to recognize this tendency within themselves, all the while being tempted to give them our opinion as to how they can correct the problem. The quickest route to a broken friendship is to step in and tell little Johnny's mother and father that they are doing a lousy job raising their child. In our honest but presumptuous attempt to help them become better parents, we focus our attention in the wrong direction, believing that if we simply tell them how to correct their mistakes they will surely listen. Nothing could be further from the truth.

If we truly want to help the child who is being sheltered then we should be thoughtful and sensitive to the needs of his parents and family, for it is something within their emotional makeup that fuels their tendency to raise a child in that manner. It is easy to believe that if we merely suggest a modification in the way a parent thinks about discipline it will accomplish the goal; however, it is those issues more closely related to their heart that hold the key to change. There are probably hundreds of reasons which could explain why parents overprotect their children, yet there are several common factors that play critical roles in providing the foundations for overprotection.

Grief

In the fall of 1984 I counseled with Bobbie and Richard, a young married couple who related a story that was all too reminiscent of the death of my brother Frankie. Jeffrey was their twenty-month-old son, whom they had hoped and prayed for since the earliest days of their marriage. He was everything they had ever dreamed—compliant, easygoing, a pleasant child with a laugh that could be heard throughout the home. He liked to sit with his dad and watch baseball on television or play catch whenever there was an opportunity. He was their only son—life could not have been more complete.

Bobbie did not pay much attention to the slight elevation in her son's temperature early one morning. She had seen this symptom many times in his older sister, Alicia, so she thought he probably had the beginnings of a cold, or maybe a baby tooth was pushing its way through. As the day progressed, so did his temperature. Baby aspirin would not curtail his fever, which was approaching 102 degrees. A tepid bath failed to stem this increase as well, and Jeffrey's skin became hot to the touch. Although his mother was responding correctly to his needs, she felt helpless as she called the doctor to explain her son's symptoms. The family physician requested to see him immediately.

By the time Bobbie arrived at the hospital, her son's body had become limp, and he had lapsed into unconsciousness. His fever had reached 105 degrees! Somewhere, possibly between his bedroom crib and the backyard slide, or while walking with his mother at the department store, he contracted bacterial meningitis. No explanation would prove sufficient to relieve the anxiety that engulfed the family over the next few hours. The hospital staff was encouraging, but Jeffrey's little body could not withstand the massive infection. His parents, who one and a half years earlier had labored together to bring their son into the world, stood at his bedside and helplessly watched him succumb to the illness. He never had a chance to break in his tiny baseball glove or grow into his oversized cap. His father's goals and aspirations for the young boy's future were gone.

In the months following their son's funeral, the response of those around Bobbie and Richard became more painful to live with than the lingering memories of Jeffrey's death. Some relatives and church members questioned why they had failed to recover from their grief within a few months of their son's death. It seemed to some of their friends that three to six months ought to be sufficient time to restore Richard and Bobbie to their former selves, yet none of these folks had ever experienced such a tragedy. Others questioned the couple's faith, hinting that a lack of trust in God was behind their inability to bounce back quickly.

Because of this lack of sensitivity, an obstacle was placed in the grief process of the deceased boy's mother and father. Instead of looking to the God they loved and to each other for their strength, they began to feel that somehow this criticism was valid. This stimulated within them a need to put on a front—to make themselves appear much happier than they truly were. This façade became unbearable to live with; however, they were caught in a bind. On the one hand, they could not be honest with their emotions for fear of rejection; and on the other hand, the more they remained silent, the more compounded their grief became.

Bobbie's greatest wish was to express her feelings to her closest friends. Also, there were moments immediately following her son's death when all she wanted to do was grab the blanket that Jeffrey loved and rush to his graveside just to rock back and forth, longing to hold him once again. In her heart she realized that her wish was impossible, yet, was it so strange that she desired her son in this fashion? At times, Richard would notice the little baseball cap that his son had worn and break into tears knowing that he would never see his boy don that cap again. Did they lack faith in God simply because their grief took longer than what others suggested was "normal"?

In an attempt to ease their confusion, I shared with them that grief is a process of emotions that is not simply left behind at the graveside, and that the well-meaning expectations of others for them to resolve their pain quickly were ill-founded and misguided. Their grief, in order for it to be brought to a healthy conclusion, should have been directed towards the son whom they had lost. Bobbie and Richard were unable to fully accomplish this because of the demands of those around them. Jeffrey's parents were denied permission to complete their last remaining moments of grief over his death and, as a result, these unresolved feelings began to cause personal conflicts within them.

In their private moments, Bobbie and Richard were experiencing emotions in addition to those of grief which hindered even further their recovery from Jeffrey's death. Richard, although he had never openly expressed this feeling to his wife, was angry with her over the loss of their son. Although he knew it was a twisted form of logic, he blamed her for failing to recognize and respond more quickly to their son's illness. With his wife beside him, he would lie awake in bed late into the night attempting to justify this emotion within himself, but he realized he could not.

While Richard struggled in silence to resolve his pain, Bobbie was involved in a struggle of her own. She was overrun with guilt. Repeatedly she said to herself, "If only I would have detected Jeffrey's symptoms earlier, I could have saved him." She realized that her self-condemnation was unjustified; however, this was her only way of expressing her remorse since she thought her husband to be unapproachable. Because Bobbie had lost touch with her husband, she began to look toward their daughter, Alicia, to regain her emotional support. In an attempt to make up for her "failure" with Jeffrey, she became overprotective of her daughter's every move.

One might ask how all of this could have happened to such a closely-knit family. To answer this question we must go back to the early stages of their grief. Those of us who have lost a loved one recognize that there is a critical period in the lives of the surviving family—those waning weeks after the funeral. During this interval of time, all of the condolences come to an end, the sympathy cards stop coming, the phone calls of encouragement cease, and the meals brought in by relatives and friends are no more. The family is alone once again. It is at this juncture when their attention, which was focused on the funeral, turns inward. This is the moment when a grieving couple such as Bobbie and Richard must find the courage for complete honesty. In a spirit of love and acceptance, each gives the other permission to express the most intimate of feelings, especially those of guilt and anger. Unfortunately, this did not happen after Jeffrey's death. For fear of how each other, friends, and family might respond, Bobbie and Richard could not be candid. The risk of further alienation was too great.

Instead of being drawn closer together, Bobbie and Richard drifted apart because their time of mourning was interrupted. They were forced to redirect their feelings toward meeting the needs of others, instead of themselves. While they should have been communicating with each other to heal their damaged emotions, each suffered alone. Their grief was trapped within them, eating away like an emotional cancer, and placing Alicia in a "glass bubble" would fail to resolve the turmoil of guilt within them.

With this in mind, we must understand that grief plays a potential role in overprotection. In and of itself, it does not directly cause parents to shelter their child; but if left unresolved, it provides the breeding ground for guilt, which is a primary contributor.

Guilt

After the death of my brother Frankie, guilt consumed the minds and hearts of my family—especially my grandfather. With his grandson gone, this emotion lured my granddad into a spirit of self-condemnation which was pervasive throughout his waking hours. Although he was absent at the time of the accident, this failed, in his mind, to relieve him of culpability. His readiness to accept full responsibility for his grandson's death became all-consuming, and he viewed himself as a failure. In a moment of time, probably of which he was not consciously aware, he quietly promised himself that he would never again become the cause of someone else's pain. Therefore, he set out to prove that he would become a better grandfather. With guilt as the foundation, his pledge altered forever the manner in which he disciplined his next grandson—me—resulting in a very overprotected child.

This emotion took its toll in the lives of other people as well. As one might expect, the driver of the bakery truck who was involved in the tragedy was placed on an alternate delivery route, far removed from my grandparents' home. Justifiably, he was never criminally charged; however, his employers thought a different work environment would be in his best interest, hoping that it would help him to recover emotionally. Unfortunately, it did not. He quit his job shortly thereafter because the lingering memories of the accident broke his will to continue.

My family wondered whatever became of that easy-going, friendly, young man. In light of the physical requirements of his former job, they thought he would be destined to play football or another contact sport because he was strong, healthy, and full of life. One afternoon, about a year after Frankie's death, my parents were grocery shopping close to their home. Upon entering the store, they noticed someone who looked familiar, but they were uncertain as to who it might be. To their surprise, it was the man who had accidentally killed their son. Few parents would ever forget the face of such a man, yet they were shocked at what they saw. His hair had turned completely white, and his youthful appearance was gone! Though they knew him to be in his late twenties, he looked decades older. He was a mere reflection of his former self. Guilt had taken its toll upon him as well.

My grandfather prided himself in his ability to be a good parent. He raised my dad to become a loving and responsible young man, and he was resolved to do the same for his grandchildren. However, because of what he perceived to be his role in the death of my brother, it was as if he had been emptied of his self-respect. Guilt would not allow him to forgive himself. Somehow, he had to set the record straight. Believing that he could make peace with himself, he showered me with the love and affection that he was unable to give Frankie. In his relentless quest to prove that he could make up for his past "failure," he allowed my environment to become too comfortable. In doing so, his self-worth was renewed; however, the long-term results within *me* were emotional pain and a low self-esteem.

Unfortunately, some of us make the same mistake as my grandfather, believing that we can soothe parental guilt by fulfilling the needs of our children. We overcompensate in how we communicate love toward them, either by not wanting to say "no" or by hovering over them lest they face any pain or discomfort. Because of this, we become ensnared in a pattern of responding to their desires in a way that will handicap them for the future. While trying to atone for our guilt, we inadvertently sacrifice discipline.

Pride

Because we have a tremendous personal investment in our children, one of the most difficult tasks we have before us is giving them the freedom to fail. This, however, can become a delicate balancing act. If we stand in the background and watch them stumble or fall, we provide them with the opportunity to increase their self-confidence by helping them realize that they have the ability to recover from their own mistakes. At the same time, however, we know that allowing them to do so may cause them to become frustrated, discouraged, and view themselves as failures—which motivates us to step in and rescue them. To equalize this issue of freedom *versus* protection, we must recognize the amount of pride within us, for it can alter the level of discipline we apply toward our children.

Recently, I was discussing this issue with a young woman in our church who is an elementary school teacher. She described to me a situation within her classroom that beautifully illustrates my point. One of her seven-year-old students, Susan, had a history of being sloppy, disorganized, and forgetful of her homework. Soon this began to affect her grades, and after the first report card, her mother, Jan, became quite concerned. Jan called to discuss her daughter's problems, and the teacher explained the cause of Susan's decline in performance. After a brief conversation, her mother promised that Susan's grades would improve. Over the course of the next few weeks, Jan's presence at the school increased greatly. Every afternoon, when she came to pick up her daughter, she would search out the teacher to be certain of Susan's homework assignment. From there, she would go directly to her little girl's school desk to secure the appropriate textbooks. There was no need for Susan to be organized in this regard because instead of requiring Susan to be responsible for her own assignments, Jan assumed all the responsibility.

After a few weeks, it became obvious to the school leadership that Jan's desire to help her daughter was only compounding Susan's difficulties. It appeared that a parent-teacher conference would be the only way to resolve Jan's overprotection. This meeting failed, however, to change her thinking. Throughout their conversation, the teacher became aware of how much Jan's pride was immersed within Susan's success. She could not bear to see her daughter's grades go down, for it was tantamount to failing herself, and Jan was not about to look bad in the eyes of others. Jan believed, erroneously, that she could prevent both of them from experiencing failure by stepping in to assume responsibility for her daughter's lack of self-discipline. Ironically, it was Jan's unwillingness to discipline Susan that resulted in her failure, because Susan was held back a grade the following year.

With this in mind, we need to recognize that pride is one of the foundations of overprotection because it promotes a self-fulfilling prophesy. When we become afraid of anything that may cause our children to experience defeat, we shelter them from potential failure, which only culminates in the likelihood that they will fail. Our constant hovering sets up a tragic chain of events, for it causes our children's self-esteem to diminish because they begin to believe themselves incapable of overcoming trials on their own. This stimulates within them a dependency upon others to help them escape from responsibility in the future. Because of this, we must not allow our pride to justify the rescuing of our children. Rather, we need to hold them accountable for their lack of self-discipline and equip them with the tools they will need to overcome life's hurdles. With love, encouragement, and reinforcement, we can increase their self-esteem and dependency upon God—which will make us *all* proud.

Unfinished Business

There are a few of us who are still emotionally charged with unresolved issues from our childhood. Someone may have intentionally hurt us, or failed to live up to our expectations, which caused us to harbor feelings of disappointment or anger. If these emotions center around the manner in which we were raised, then we have probably developed a negative response to our mother and father's style of parenting, which could affect the way we discipline our own children. This is most common if our parents' "discipline" was extreme or abusive.

One of the most difficult jobs before me as a Minister and Marriage and Family Counselor is to report parents for the abuse of their children. Fortunately, if I am able to catch the situation early enough, I can prevent irreparable damage from occurring of either a physical or emotional nature. Too many times, however, I become aware of the abuse long after the children have grown into adulthood. Surviving through this living hell does not always guarantee that their emotional life has been healed. Usually, it has not. The scars have been etched so deeply within their character that it often affects the manner in which they discipline their children; this also provides a foundation for overprotection.

Linda was a beautiful young woman who came to me for counseling over three years ago with problems related to child discipline. This was puzzling because she had two good-natured little girls and a husband who was a devoted family man. It would have appeared, based upon her family, that she had everything in life going her way. Yet, she was very adverse to biblical methods of correction. Linda described that she grew up in a fractured home which was twice broken because of divorce. After the first divorce, her mother fell in love with the minister of a church in the town where she lived, and after a long courtship, they decided to get married. Linda was seven years old. Because of the physical abuse that occurred in the previous marriage, and the years of separation that ensued, she never developed a lasting relationship with her natural father. Her mother's new husband, Bob, became the only father she ever knew.

Like most gradeschoolers, Linda had her moments of defiance. One evening, while her mother was out shopping, she became exceptionally rebellious, which required Bob's discipline. Instead of correcting her in a biblical manner, he began to fondle her, threatening to tell Linda's mother of her rebelliousness if she spoke a word of what he was doing. His intimidation and threats of reprisal lasted for several years, with Linda's mom unaware of the abuse. As Linda reached junior high age, the severity of the abuse increased. Using fear to maintain secrecy, Bob began to have sexual intercourse with his eleven-year-old stepdaughter as a form of "discipline" for her disobedience. Night after night, Linda would plead with her mother not to leave for Bible study or run errands because she feared the consequences if she did. Her mother, however, thought Linda was insecure, not realizing the terror she was going through.

The sexually abusive relationship between Linda and her stepfather continued for two years, until she was thirteen, when Bob was reported to the authorities by his wife, who finally became aware of the situation. Linda never fully recovered from her past. When she appeared in my office for counseling, fifteen years had elapsed since the abuse stopped.

With her stepfather's abuse as a foundation, Linda formed very negative opinions about a parent's role in the correction of children. Unknowingly she had linked discipline with abuse. These two concepts had become so intertwined throughout her childhood that to her they were indistinguishable. Thus, her misconception, in combination with the resentment she harbored toward Bob, caused her to pledge that she would never follow in his footsteps. When her own children misbehaved, Linda could not bring herself to correct them, let alone spank them. She could not make herself discipline her girls, even though she knew it was in their best interests.

As one might assume, Linda's response to her abusive past was to be expected; however, she was losing control of her home—her two daughters were becoming unruly. How was I to assist her in becoming free from this dilemma? I could have taken an educational approach, and taught her the proper techniques of child discipline. But she was well-read on the subject, having attended seminars as well. All of this information would have failed to produce the comfort she desired. Another approach might have been an analytical one—helping her to sift through the underlying reasons why she was struggling. This idea also would have brought little relief. These methods are not without merit because, depending upon the circumstances and the individual, they could become valuable tools in helping to alleviate a client's pain. In Linda's case, however, she had but one solution to bring about healing in her life—forgiveness.

It has been said that resentment is "my demand that you feel guilty," and Linda had spent most of her adult life demanding that Bob ought to feel guilty. Because of what he had done to her, she not only wanted him to feel guilty, but wanted him to take responsibility for her resentment as well. Somehow, she had convinced herself that if she could force him to take ownership of these emotions, that she could become free of her own bitterness. However, Bob had long since rationalized away his own guilt, and had unjustifiably forgiven himself of what he had done. Because of this, he felt no need to share in the responsibility of resolving Linda's emotional conflict. Though her anger towards him was legitimate (and certainly understandable), she failed to realize that God had not given her the privilege to become judge, jury, and executioner in his life. Her goal to punish him would fail to resolve the bitterness within her.

Some people would take my suggestion of forgiveness to be foolish. They would say that at the very least, she had every right to hate him for the rest of her life. Though Bob deserved to receive just punishment for his actions, Linda deceived herself into believing that she would find solace through hatred. If only she could have found inspiration in the words of Oswald Chambers when he commented on forgiveness from Matthew 5:39: "But I say unto you, That ye resist not evil; but whosoever shall smite thee on thy right cheek, turn to him the other also."

These verses reveal the humiliation of being a Christian. Naturally, if a man does not hit back, it is because he is a coward; but spiritually if a man does not hit back, it is a manifestation of the Son of God in him. When you are insulted, you must not only not resent it, but make it an occasion to exhibit the Son of God. You cannot imitate the disposition of Jesus; it is either there or it is not. To the saint personal insult becomes the occasion of revealing the incredible sweetness of the Lord Jesus.

The teaching of the Sermon on the Mount is not—Do your Duty, but—Do what is not your duty. It is not your duty to go the second mile, to turn the other cheek, but Jesus says if we are His disciples we shall always do these things. There will be no spirit of—"Oh, well, I cannot do any more, I have been so misrepresented and misunderstood." Every time I insist upon my rights, I hurt the Son of God; whereas I can prevent Jesus from being hurt if I take the blow myself. That is the meaning of filling up that which is behind of the afflictions of Christ. The disciple realizes that it is his Lord's honor that is at stake in his life, not his own honor.

Never look for right in the other man, but never cease to be right yourself. We are always looking for justice; the teaching of the Sermon on the Mount is—Never look for justice, but never cease to give it.[1]

Linda had become so embittered that she continued to insist upon her right to retaliate against Bob. What she failed to recognize, however, was her resentfulness towards God. She refused to accept my suggestion that her respect for the Lord had become tainted through her stepfather's abuse. After all, he was a "minister," one of God's "ambassadors," a "model" for all to live by. Yet knowing what he had done to her and watching him preach on Sunday mornings made her sick. Her reverence for God had been corrupted because Bob was a phony. She could not forgive her earthly father because she held her heavenly Father to blame.

Is it any wonder that Linda was unwilling to follow biblical principles for the discipline of her children? Her understanding of God had been formulated in the light of Bob's abuse, and she was not about to entrust the care of her daughters to either of them. Unfinished business, the foundation for her overprotection, was the repercussion of her abuse and her refusal to forgive.

----

[1] Taken from *My Utmost for His Highest* by Oswald Chambers. Copyright 1935, Dodd, Mead, & Company, Inc. Used by permission.

4

A Reality
Too Painful

ONCE A CHILD WHO has lived in an overprotective environment reaches preschool age, he begins to adopt a much different perspective of his surroundings than that of his immediate family. From his parents' point of view, they have lovingly provided for his needs, making sure that he was happy, warm, and fed. Also, they may have taken many opportunities to give him whatever his little heart desired, but what's the harm? Probably very little, they said to themselves. However, as their child develops beyond infancy, he attains a greater understanding of his surroundings, learning that there is more to living than a full stomach and a dry diaper. If, as a toddler, his family continues to accommodate his every whim, he will become conditioned to expect that this is normal. Thus, when this is combined with his natural ability to be selfish, he adopts a much different perspective of life—that the world, and those therein, exist to serve him.

Mothers and fathers sometimes see this attitude reflected in their own child's behavior when he gives orders to other family members. Demanding this or that, he expects that we should be grateful and sing high praises to his name for doing so, but we all accept that he does not have a realistic view of what the world is like. Yet if those who are entrusted with his care continue to reinforce his foolish idea that the world revolves around him, then he will surmise that life is a free ride, devoid of work. With this in mind, we no longer have a child who is simply overprotected, but one who is developing a spoiled nature. This is not accomplished, however, simply due to the hovering nature of his parents or relatives. Rather, it is a combination of *their* overindulgence and *his* self-centeredness. His naturally selfish mentality combined with the continual experience being catered to has caused him to conclude that life is a road paved with easy work and one-sided relationships—all the ingredients for a disastrous upbringing. Eventually, his unrealistic manner of relating to people will become a reality too painful for him and others to live with.

The overprotected child evolves into a spoiled child, primarily, through a permissive parenting style. If there is one good quality where permissive parents tend to excel, it is in their ability to show love towards their children. However, they struggle with the ability to follow through in discipline, causing the child to believe that his parents do not really mean what they say. Children, especially under the age of nine, think literally. They do not possess the higher cognitive reasoning power of an adult. As a result, they do not understand contradictions. The old saying, "Do as I say, not as I do," is a foreign thought to him, for if a parent says one thing and does another, the child will always believe what he sees. To him, that *is* reality. Thus, regardless of threats and pleadings, when Mom and Dad fail to *demonstrate* that there are consequences to disobedience, their child will grow up believing that reality is having his own way. Spoiling a child, therefore, can be directly expressed through overindulging him; however, it can also be indirectly expressed by the following disciplinary environments we as parents set within the home.

Permissiveness

One of my father's greatest pastimes is deep sea fishing. We who live in Southern California recognize that anytime during the year we can catch kelp bass or halibut, but those hardy souls who desire big game fish must wait until summer when albacore are in season. Catching this member of the tuna family is sort of a mixed blessing. As you set out to sea, bobbing up and down upon the waves causes you to become seasick. The nausea dissipates, however, once the albacore bites the hook, which is somewhat like reeling in a runaway mule. You can have more fun than one can imagine as the fish takes you around the boat several times, but once you've completed your day's fishing, it's back to leaning over the rail of the boat. After this ordeal, your only wish is to be back on dry land. You begin to experience great relief as the harbor comes into view, but after the boat is in the dock, it takes over an hour for your head to stop spinning. Once your body has been assaulted in this fashion, the last item on your priority list is the gutting, skinning, and filleting of a smelly tuna. Upon completion of this task, every cat in the community loves you; however, your wife has disowned you, refusing to speak until you have buried your clothes and bathed three times. The goal behind all of this self-torture (in case you were wondering) is the canning of the tuna, preserving it for numerous future feasts.

My mother spent hours in meticulous preparation for this event. Not only did she require that the fish be cleaned properly, but that the canning jars be washed, rinsed, and sterilized with boiling water. The albacore had to be cut up into pieces small enough to fit the size of the jars, and once placed inside, there could be no scraps of fish or residue remaining on the rim, lest any bacteria should grow. The canning lids had to be sterilized as well, so that a tight seal could form on top of the jar. Once she had completed this marathon task, it was essential that the fish be cooked in the proper environment—a pressure cooker—for the prescribed amount of time. The jars full of fish were then transferred to a table or counter top to cool. If she had done her job well, the final stage of the process should be successful—the indentation on top of the lid should depress, signifying a vacuum seal.

To veteran home canners, this procedure which I have just described is nothing new. You realize that it must be adhered to every time, exactly the same way, with no shortcuts. If it is done incorrectly the risk of serious illness through food poisoning is severe. As a gradeschooler, I believed my mother's routine for the canning of food was archaic—too much effort. I thought to myself, "Why be so disciplined? Let's be more permissive and cut a few corners to save ourselves a great deal of work." Can you imagine what would have happened if Mother let me can fish the way I wanted to do it? She would have been risking the well-being of many just to please one. Fortunately, my mom was unwilling to indulge me in my foolishness. She would not surrender her traditional method of canning food, for she realized the consequences upon her family.

The child with the spoiled nature is always looking at life from the easy chair. The "Life of Riley" is his favorite television re-run, and whatever feels the most comfortable is the path he will travel, even if he has to adopt an undisciplined lifestyle to get there. He may whine, pout, or scream to get his own way, but he fails to understand that someone is going to have to pay the consequences for his irresponsibility. Because of this, the manner in which his parents respond to his self-serving nature is critical to his long-term character development. Some parents are permissive for the sake of avoiding an argument. Others are permissive so that their child will like them. But for the sake of his spiritual and emotional health, they must not become lenient in their godly application of discipline, because if they are unwilling to hold him accountable for his behavior, he will trust that someone else will assume the consequences.

Rescuing

If the disciplinary environment within the home remains permissive as a child gets older, he will grow in his expectation that someone will rescue him from his mistakes. His belief that life is devoid of the painful consequences of irresponsibility and misbehavior only compounds his distortion of what the world is like, causing him to become too dependent upon others. For this reason, a major stumbling block will be placed in his path toward maturity because he will fail to learn that maturity only comes through a confrontation with reality. Rescuing him from reality merely circumvents this from occurring.

In my younger days as a counselor, I was approached by the mother of three children who found this concept most difficult to accept. Though her chief complaint was of a marital nature, we were soon to find out that the core of her personal difficulties centered around her tendency to rescue her children from irresponsibility. Little did she know how difficult it would be for her to change this permissive style of parenting.

Her twenty-seven-year-old daughter had suffered the greatest repercussions of Mom's overprotection, with Dad the recipient of most of the consequences. Though she had been out of the home for almost ten years, she was still emotionally and physically dependent upon her folks. Since she had moved away, her mom had paid the majority of her monthly house payments, primarily because of her daughter's unwillingness to seek employment. Furthermore, one night around 1:00 A.M., the daughter phoned her parents from an emergency call-box on the freeway. She was stranded because the engine of her car had overheated and died. Of course, it was Dad who was summoned to tow her home. Rolling out of bed half asleep, he thought his daughter's predicament to be rather puzzling because he had just rebuilt her car's engine one year before. In the morning, as he began to investigate the problem thoroughly, he was surprised to learn that there was no oil in the engine! As he pulled the oil pan off the bottom of the motor, all that remained was a sticky substance resembling cooking molasses. He had reminded his daughter on numerous occasions to put oil and water in her car, so he inquired of her how this could have happened. Her reply, "Well, I just didn't think about doing it!" No use lecturing her on the value of possessions, Dad said to himself, for she has been this way ever since she was a child. Because Dad knew that a further discussion of the issue would be in vain, he remained silent and spent the hundreds of dollars it took to rebuild his daughter's engine—which he did himself—again.

Of course, this is not an indictment against those of the feminine gender who are unable to repair cars. I know men who can't tell the difference between a head gasket and a hat rack. But is it any wonder why this young woman had become so irresponsible? To answer this question fully, we must recognize that the permissive environment of the home had caused her to become spoiled. She had been taught throughout her childhood that she could depend upon others to accomplish her work. Thus, she never grew into maturity because her mother was unwilling to confront her with reality—that she accept responsibility and not be rescued from the consequences when she neglected to do so.

Submission

Once a child has grown accustomed to being rescued from his misbehavior, it is only a matter of time before he concludes that he will not be held accountable when he rebels against authority. His belief that he is only answerable to himself creates turmoil within his life, and all those who must associate with him, because his self-governing nature becomes impossible to live with. His sense of autonomy causes others to reject him, which culminates in a low self-esteem. Furthermore, his independent spirit blinds him from recognizing the importance of being submissive to the needs of others, which is a fundamental ingredient of all success-ful relationships. As a result, the spoiled child will be unsuc-cessful in his attempts to develop interpersonal closeness and will fall short in placing himself under the subjection of God. The apostle Peter recognized the importance of sub-mission when he wrote in 1 Peter 5:5–6: "Likewise you that are younger be subject to the elders. Clothe yourselves, all of you, with humility toward one another, for 'God opposes the proud, but gives grace to the humble'. Humble (submit) yourselves therefore under the mighty hand of God, that in due time he may exalt you" (parentheses mine). In light of this passage, Edwin A. Blum shares from the *Expositor's Bible Commentary* important implications for the way in which we raise our children.

> "Clothe yourselves" *(egkombosasthe)* is a rare word that re-fers to a slave putting on an apron before serving. So Chris-tians are to imitate their Lord, who girded himself and served (John 13:4–17). The reason for humility is based on a text from Proverbs (3:34; cf. James 4:6) that states God's provision of grace to the submissive and God's opposition to the proud. The verbs are present tenses, with something of the timeless character of a proverb, and stress that these actions are God's constant activity.[1]

These verses are directed towards all of us as Chris-tians; however, they hold particular importance for those of us who are parents. As we watch our children develop, we become keenly aware of their unwillingness to submit to instruction. They kick and scream at any self-improvement project and rebel at every turn. Due to their immaturity, they do not understand that the ability to be submissive is dependent upon humility.

Humility

The spoiled child does not see the importance of humility because he views himself as the center of his universe. He is not *to serve*, but rather *to be served* by others, and possibly even by God. Most of us are repulsed by people who view themselves from such a lofty perch; furthermore, God is not our personal bellhop. As one could imagine, a child who adopts such a lifestyle will suffer greatly with his self-worth and interpersonal relationships, because those around him are not about to relate with him on his terms. With this in mind, we must recognize that because our children are naturally inclined toward selfishness, God entrusts us to clothe them with a spirit of humility and service. If our children fail to incorporate this principle within their character, they will be unable to reflect the nature of Jesus Christ because, due to their lack of submission, they will be standing in direct opposition to His will.

This lack of humility is a developmental milestone that is overcome within our children's lives when we allow them to experience the inconvenience associated with serving others. When I was first baptized at the age of sixteen, it was the custom of the church where I was a member to hold a foot-washing and communion service once each quarter. When I first became aware of this practice, I said to myself that there was no way I would humble myself and submit to wash some old man's dirty feet. This whole idea was emotionally repulsive to me, which caused me to rebel. It wasn't until I read the Gospel of John, chapter 13, however, that I began to respect the meaning behind this ceremony. I learned that humility was a form of submission—a relinquishing of my own authority for the benefit of all those concerned—an act of service. This is a completely foreign thought to children, and it pains them greatly when we attempt to develop within them an attitude of selflessness. Their natural response is to be self-serving, and ward off any attempts on our part to have them give of themselves. Every evening, my daughter Nicole hoists her dinner plate three feet into the air because she is so afraid that her fifteen-month-old sister will steal a speck of food. There can be a whole platter full of food remaining on the dinner table, but the only word that Nicole understands is "mine." We didn't teach her to be so stingy, it's just a natural part of her character. As a result, my wife and I ask Nicky at times to give some of her meal to Laura just to teach her an attitude of self-sacrifice. We realize that even though this may upset her, she will become much less selfish as a result.

With this in mind, we must not run the risk of spoiling our children by rescuing them from being submissive and humbling themselves to the needs of others. It may require that we allow them to experience some minor level of discomfort or emotional pain as we equip them to become more self-sacrificing. It is worth the cost because the overcoming of this milestone equips them to meet the needs of others as they grow older. This element of our children's character is one of the keys in helping them to establish successful interpersonal relationships. As they learn to submit first to their parents, they will begin to extend it to other family members, the community, and ultimately toward God.

Overdependence

Unfortunately, a child will progress down the road of a spoiled nature if one or more of those who love him perpetuate his overprotective or permissive environment. Giving in to his selfish desires only encourages him to become more demanding, causing others to avoid him. Furthermore, instead of being equipped with the spiritual, emotional, and physical tools necessary to confront the trials and demands of life, the "wall of protection" continues to shield him from confronting and overcoming these realities. With selfishness and overprotection at the core of his personality, the groundwork is set for a life full of personal heartache and pain. Soon, the spoiled child will begin to experience rejection and an overwhelming sense of incompetence because he has relied upon others to pave an easy road of life for him.

I had mentioned earlier that when I was a youngster, it was my grandfather who enabled me to adopt such a faulty perception of the world. Together, we made my childhood fun, free of anything requiring work. Most of my days were consumed in playing with my friends, which was much more enjoyable than doing my schoolwork. My mom and dad, however, had other ideas and wanted me to learn and receive good grades. So in order to have the best of both worlds, I found the perfect alternative—I would enjoy myself immediately after school and then watch television as my grandfather gave me the answers to my homework assignments. He was more than willing to accommodate me because he wanted my approval as well as the high marks my parents had desired. Therefore, I would sit and watch cartoons while Granddad responded to my questions, "What is two plus two? The first president of the United States? The Declaration of Independence?" If the questions were multiple choice, I would tell him the choices and he would tell me the correct answers. If the questions were true or false, he would tell me what was true and what was false.

As expected, one could foresee the consequences upon me for being rescued from doing my own homework. There was very little learning involved in my study habits; therefore, I was incapable of responding when it came time to take the test. With my grandfather's assistance, I received straight As on my homework assignments, and with my shifty pair of eyes on test day, I pulled an overall grade point average of a B. Since everything looked good on paper, it didn't matter to me that I was becoming uneducated and ill-equipped to deal with my future. I had mistakenly believed that we had the unbeatable system—until my grandfather died when I was fourteen. With him gone, what was I to do?

How was I to function without him paving an easy road of life for me?

Although my grandfather loved me deeply and had great aspirations for my future, he could not foresee the aftermath of my spoiled nature. If he had known that his permissiveness would culminate in a grandson who was insecure and incapable of overcoming the challenges of life, he would have chosen to let me suffer the consequences of my laziness and disciplined me for my selfish and demanding nature. Unfortunately, this did not occur. The bubble of overprotection had burst—I was on my own.

Ultimately, there will come a time in every child's life when he will have to confront life on his own. Someday, the permissive environment in which he may have been raised will be stripped away from him, thereby forcing him to become emancipated. *It is inevitable that this will occur.* It will happen, possibly due to the death of the person who overprotected him, by his fear of failure, or by others calling him to a new level of accountability. Irrespective of how this occurs, the spoiled child will be confronted with reality—that he is responsible for his own decisions and behavior. No longer will others step in and rescue him from his irresponsibility. No longer will the wall of protection be maintained to shield him from the unpleasant circumstances of life. No longer will people allow themselves to be coerced and manipulated into responding to his selfish demands. Whether he is fourteen or forty, this truth comes as a great shock to him. Since he has grown overdependent upon his sheltered environment for success, the absence of it places his self-esteem in great jeopardy. He recognizes that in the absence of the person who overprotected him, he has the respect of few others. Furthermore, he has grave doubts about his ability to live up to the standards of what others expect of him. As a result, this becomes a reality too painful to live with. Somewhere, somehow, he will strive to regain the integrity which he has lost—in search of self-worth.

---

[1] Taken from *Expositor's Bible Commentary: Vol. 12.* Edited by Frank E. Gaebelin (General Editor). Copyright 1981 by the Zondervan corporation. Used by permission.

5

In Search of
Self-Worth

THE SPOILED CHILD TRAVELS into his adolescence at a terrible disadvantage because he lacks the spiritual and emotional equipment to successfully confront life's demands, trials, and failures. He feels incapable of adequately responding to what the world expects of him, for he has been sheltered from doing so throughout his childhood. As a result, this leads to a massive infusion of insecurity and a low self-esteem. His fear of failure consumes his daily thoughts, causing him to doubt himself and become afraid of others. In the truest sense of the term, he is far too emotionally crippled to integrate into the mainstream of daily living. Therefore, in a desperate and vain attempt to bolster his ego, the spoiled child alters his behavior, life-style, mannerisms, and attitudes to look good and seek the approval of others—in search of self-worth.

This ability to change one's character reminds me of one of God's little known creatures, the chameleon. The chameleon is found most often in Africa and is a member of the lizard family. He is a rather odd fellow whose four feet point in opposite directions and who would never win a beauty contest. Neither is he quick on his feet, making him rather vulnerable to attack. Despite his defenseless nature however, he has survived throughout the centuries because of his unique ability to adapt when confronted with danger.

As the chameleon goes about his daily affairs he is always mindful of his predators. When he is threatened, he changes the color of his skin to closely resemble his immediate surroundings—thereby rendering himself secure. If he is walking along on the stem of a plant with green leaves, he instantly changes his skin pigmentation to become camouflaged when he believes his life to be in peril. Green, brown, yellow, even speckled—it doesn't matter where he is or who he is with, his disguise serves to maintain his security.

Somewhat in the same manner, the spoiled adolescent adapts himself to the people and places that threaten his self-esteem. Due to his overprotective childhood, his ego has become so insecure that he guards it just like a thirsty man walking in the desert would protect the only cup of water remaining in his canteen. What little self-worth he has left is so precious to him that he is unwilling to take any risks which might further jeopardize what remains. For this reason, he maintains what is left of his self-concept by scanning his environment for interpersonal relationships that appear threatening, refusing to assert himself for fear of being rejected. Not wanting to risk the disapproval of those around him (especially his friends), he takes on some of their characteristics or life-styles in order to fit in. If those around him use foul language, he may use foul language. If they get drunk, he may get drunk, and so forth. In essence, he searches for self-worth by making a pre-judgement of how others think of him. Based upon what he concludes, he alters his life-style and mannerisms to meet their expectations, hoping all along that he will find approval and a positive self-image.

To some degree, all of us conform to the expectations of others. Some time ago Prince Charles and Princess Diana of England visited the United States, and I was amazed at the pomp and circumstance surrounding their stay. Guests and attendants who were invited to the royal gathering had to attend a special school for two days just to be educated in the proper way of addressing the royal couple. This was necessary to avoid such comments as, "Hi Chuck and Di, how ya doing?" Such remarks are obviously not in keeping with the degree of dignity afforded those of such high honor; therefore, the men who were invited were taught to nod at the head, and the women to bend at the knee or curtsy. It would be foolish to suggest that someone is insecure simply because he modifies his behavior to meet this type of expectation. The ability to adjust ourselves to meet the demands of a special occasion is not at issue here. Rather, we are talking about letting our goodness be defined by others instead of God, which prompts us to mold our attitudes and behavior around what will please them. In search of self-worth, we become dependent upon their appraisal of who we are in order to feel good about ourselves.

This reminds me of a sixteen-year-old girl with whom I spoke in 1984, who had been raised in a home with a sheltered environment. Mom and Dad loved her so much that they stepped in, on her behalf, every time she faced a difficult problem in life. This was their attempt to make her successful; however, fighting their daughter's battles throughout her childhood only compounded her inability to make decisions. She had grown so dependent upon her parents in this regard that once she found herself in high school she doubted her every move, lacking the self-confidence to make mature decisions on her own. Not wanting to make a mistake and incur the possibility of rejection, she would not stand up for herself even when confronted with what she knew to be wrong. As a result of her lack of self-confidence, her behavior began to fluctuate around that of her friends and what she thought would please them. Fearing rejection, she set aside her Christian values and succumbed to their peer pressure.

When I spoke with this young lady, she was about to deliver her first baby. The father of the child, who had stated all along that he loved his girlfriend, abandoned her once he found out that she was pregnant. He had told her many times how beautiful she was, which gave her the self-esteem she had always wanted, yet, due to his lack of commitment, her heart was broken and the feelings of inadequacy returned. What confused her was how all of this could have happened. Oh, not in the sense that she was uneducated about human sexuality, but rather, how she could have allowed herself to get into such a predicament. It would have been a mistake for her to conclude that she was merely the victim of peer pressure. Although this was partially to blame, the core of her difficulty was centered in how she developed her self-worth.

With this in mind, the life of this young woman clearly demonstrates how easily children can learn to acquire their self-esteem from the wrong sources. The overprotection of children initiates this process because it causes them to rest their self-confidence at the feet of the one who is overprotecting them instead of within themselves and God. Their self-esteem has become anchored in sand, and they will find it easily shaken as they enter into the troubled waters of adolescence. The temptation to begin drawing their self-worth from their peers will be hard to resist. Like the chameleon, they may conform to their environment to seek security.

Not only does the spoiled adolescent alter his life-style in search of self-worth, but he rests too heavily upon it as a guarantee for success. Without a doubt, children and adults with a low self-esteem run a far greater chance at failing in what they do than those who have a positive self-concept. However, the presence of a healthy self-concept is not a sure sign of success either, and relying upon it as a prerequisite for prosperity leaves God out of the process.

Both the Old and New Testaments are full of examples where God took the most insecure individual, and through His power, transformed him into a completely new person. Take for instance, the life of Moses. In the third and fourth chapters of the book of Exodus, we have God recruiting Moses, one of the most insecure people you would ever meet, to help free the nation of Israel from the bondage of Pharaoh. In Exodus 3:10–11 God begins His conversation with Moses by saying, " 'Come, I will send you to Pharaoh that you may bring forth my people, the sons of Israel, out of Egypt.' But Moses said to God, 'Who am I that I should go to Pharaoh, and bring the sons of Israel out of Egypt?' " At this moment, let's pause and imagine ourselves in Moses' position. He was a fugitive from justice because as a young man, he had ambushed and killed an Egyptian taskmaster who was abusing one of the Hebrew slaves. Furthermore, he had been a shepherd throughout most of his adult life, acquiring few leadership skills. With this as his background, it is no wonder that he felt reluctant at the magnitude of God's request.

Because of his insecurity, Moses began a debate with God as to whether or not he was qualified to be a success at this job. He asked God by what authority he was to speak with Pharaoh, realizing that his name alone would be insufficient to persuade the King of Egypt to release the Israelites. God said that His name was "I Am," but this failed to help Moses feel more secure. Again, Moses tried to convince the Lord that he would be better off in another line of work, by saying, "Oh, my Lord, I am not eloquent, either hereto or since thou hast spoken to thy servant; but I am slow of speech and tongue." The Lord was not persuaded by this argument either, and made one more attempt to convince Moses that He would be with him, teaching him what he was to do and say. Finally, in desperation, Moses said "Oh, my Lord, send, I pray, some other person."

For those who struggle with their self-concept, Moses' life should be a source of great encouragement. He began his adulthood as a man who struggled with his self-esteem, and who visualized the likelihood of success resting only with himself. In his search for self-worth, he relied upon his own resourcefulness for the power to conquer life's hurdles, having very little confidence in God's ability to transform him into something better. Yet, because of the Lord, Moses is regarded as one of the great patriarchs of the Old Testament, his changed life giving dramatic testimony to God's handiwork.

One might ask how Moses became so insecure. If anyone within God's Word could ever be regarded as a spoiled child, Moses would be the most likely candidate. Although he was the son of Hebrew parents, he was raised in the lap of luxury in Pharaoh's household. From the day that Pharaoh's daughter found baby Moses in a reed basket along the river's edge, he had the good life at his fingertips. He was overprotected from the very beginning, and whatever his little heart desired, Pharaoh's servants were quick to respond. His toughest conflict throughout his childhood was the decision of when and where he wanted his next meal to be served. In addition, Moses developed a warped concept of interpersonal relationships and confrontation, because after all, who had the courage to honestly challenge his authority and disagree with him or anyone within Pharaoh's household? Considering the fine leader he turned out to be, there can be no doubt that it was God who completely transformed his life, despite his shortcomings.

As in the life of Moses, the key to success does not rest solely within our self-concept. If it did, Moses would have been a miserable failure. He looked upon himself as completely inadequate to respond to God's will, yet the Lord knew otherwise. The Bible teaches that no matter what kind of life we may lead, or how we may look at ourselves, God is in the life-changing business. God's willingness to change our lives from the unlovely to the beautiful is clearly taught by the apostle Paul in Romans 12:1-2 which says:

I appeal to you therefore, brethren, by the mercies of God, to present your bodies as a living sacrifice, holy and acceptable to God, which is your spiritual worship. Do not be conformed to this world but be transformed by the renewal of your mind, that you may prove what is the will of God, what is good and acceptable and perfect.

In verse 2, the word "transformed" comes from the Greek word *Metamorphoo* (*meta*—to change, and *morphe*—form). When Paul says "be transformed" he is stressing that as Christians we can undergo a complete change in our character (self-concept) through the power of God. This word *metamorphoo* should be very familiar to most of us because from it we get our English word "metamorphosis". Children understand this word as well, because they closely associate it with the life of a caterpillar whose form is changed into a butterfly. Boys and girls question, however, how one of God's ugliest creatures can become one of His most beautiful. They are taught that somehow God implanted within the tiny brain of each caterpillar how vital it is to change from his old life. This metamorphosis is not without a great deal of effort, however, because it does not happen by magic. In order to make the transformation to a butterfly, the caterpillar must first be willing to disregard his present appearance and give up his old life in search of a new one. If he is willing to take refuge in the proper environment (a cocoon), his new identity will be complete.

Whether it is that of the lowly caterpillar or of Moses, every life can be changed. We too, can undergo a transformation from our old nature. But before this will occur, we must be willing to allow our identity to be defined by God instead of ourselves or others, because the opinions of the world and those around us can fluctuate from moment to moment, causing our identity to fluctuate as well. If we take refuge in and entrust ourselves to His Word and what it defines as a whole person, then we will find the self-worth and confidence we are seeking.

For this reason, parents need to help their children search for a positive self-image in their relationship with God. The Bible teaches that God manifests Himself in three separate and distinct personalities . . . God the Father . . . Jesus His Son . . . and the Holy Spirit. Maurice Wagner in his excellent book entitled *The Sensation of Being Somebody* has shared how all three of God's personalities are involved in the development of self-esteem.[1] Self-esteem has three dimensions of its own—belonging, worth, and competence. Each of these are linked together with one of God's personalities in the building of our children's identity.

THE NATURE OF GOD IN BUILDING SELF-ESTEEM

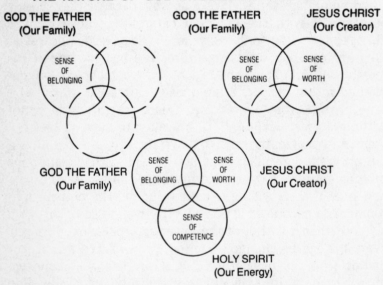

Sense Of Belonging and God The Father

God the Father helps us to feel a sense of belonging because we are members of *His* family. We are not an island unto ourselves, functioning independently from the rest of the family. We as brothers and sisters in Christ look out for each other, sacrificing our time, talent, and resources to help in time of need. When we are burdened physically, emotionally, or spiritually, members of God's family are there to help lighten that burden (Gal. 6:2). We respond in this way because we are motivated by our Father's love, and as a result, this common bond gives us security.

While watching the news early one evening, I couldn't help but be touched emotionally as I witnessed the devastation brought about by a tornado that literally destroyed an entire community in Pennsylvania. While a little girl's doll lay virtually untouched in her front yard, only a concrete slab remained of the home where she once lived. This sight is all too familiar throughout many parts of the country each year, and except for those who suffered directly, I, like many other Americans, continued to eat my supper without thinking any further about what I was watching. What is most memorable about that event was not the actual catastrophe, but the response of a few to those who were in need. As some began to bury their dead, others scrambled to state and federal agencies to begin the long and tedious process of securing loans to finance the reconstruction of new homes. Frustrations mounted as the weeks went by with no apparent financial help in sight. Yet quietly, and without any fanfare, the Amish community abandoned their own personal commitments and devoted themselves to the rebuilding project. Without architects or blueprints, houses were quickly reconstructed. To the praise of homeowners and building inspectors alike, parents and children were once again securely in their homes.

Our egos would lead us to believe that we can pull ourselves up by our own bootstraps, but in reality, we are all dependent upon others to become complete human beings. Those Pennsylvania townspeople hold the Amish in high esteem today because the Amish know how to build self-esteem in others through a sense of belonging, love, and support.

Sense of Worth and Jesus Christ

Jesus Christ develops our self-esteem by giving us a sense of worth. He is continually affirming us as persons of value. The degree to which Jesus loves us is best demonstrated by His own words in John 15:12–13 when He said:

> This is my commandment that you love one another as I have loved you. Greater love has no man than this, that a man lay down his life for his friends.

There are few modern-day parallels from which we can draw to illustrate the amount of love required for a person to literally sacrifice himself so that others may live. The finest example I know comes from a youth minister whose church I attended as a young man. Like most young men in the late 1960s, he sat anxiously as the lottery drum began to spin—anxious, not to see whether he was to be the winner of a million dollars, but rather what military draft number he would be assigned after his eighteenth birthday. His number was drawn; it was in the low twenties, which virtually guaranteed that he would spend the next two years of his life fighting the war in Viet Nam.

Throughout his tour of duty he always seemed to be one of the lucky ones. When one of his best friends was killed, he lay alongside of him in that muddy rice paddy untouched. But then, while engaged in combat late one evening, a small piece of tubular steel, not much bigger than your forearm, came flying into the bunker where he and his buddies were staying. The hand grenade landed between him and one of his friends. Though he was fully capable of jumping out of the bunker to save himself, his friend was immobilized and trapped. Without hesitation, he grabbed a dirty old mattress that the soldiers used to sleep on and threw himself upon the grenade. Instantly, he realized that he was still alive! The grenade was a dud!

This story sounds like the stuff from which Hollywood

movies are made. But this was no fairy tale, and neither is Jesus when He says that He considers us such good friends that He was willing to make the supreme sacrifice—death—so that we might have life. Like my former youth minister, our Lord could have removed Himself from His moment of death, but for our sake, He chose not to. The fact that He was willing to give up His very life for us demonstrates the degree to which He cherishes and respects us, thereby elevating our sense of worth to a new level, far beyond what the world can offer.

Sense of Competence And The Holy Spirit

The Holy Spirit gives us a sense of competence because he enables us to do the Father's work. This enabling is manifest, in part, through spiritual gifts, which is God's way of equipping us to accomplish His goals for the church. As we walk in the Spirit, there is a tremendous sense of being used by Him. Being God's representative increases our self-esteem because we are achieving something meaningful for Him and for His family.

Working to achieve His will for the family of God, and being successful at it, impacts greatly upon how we feel about ourselves. But it does not stand alone. We may accept the fact that God the Father gives us a sense of belonging, and we may acknowledge that we have worth because Jesus died for us, but at the same time, if we believe that we are incompetent, then our self-esteem will remain stagnate until we *exercise* His will. Accomplishing this is not limited to our participation within the local church, however. The apostle Paul wrote in 2 Corinthians 5:20:

So we are ambassadors for Christ, God making his appeal through us . . . .

As a member of God's family, our role goes beyond teaching a Sunday school class, repainting the outside of the fellowship hall, or becoming a church leader. It is extended to reaching the lost for Christ, which is not limited to a particular spiritual gift. God has entrusted us with a portion of His creative power in that we are empowered by the Holy Spirit to help others become new creations (reconciled) in Him. As Paul stated earlier, beginning in the seventeenth verse;

> Therefore, if any one is in Christ, he is a new creation; the old has passed away, behold, the new has come. All this is from God, who through Christ reconciled us to himself and gave us the ministry of reconciliation; that is, in Christ God was reconciling the world to himself, not counting their trespasses against them, and entrusting to us the message of reconciliation.

With this in mind, there is no greater sense of competence and boost for our self-esteem than allowing ourselves to be used by the Holy Spirit in creating a new member of God's family.

Because our sense of belonging, worth, and competence depends upon our relationship with God, we need to teach our children that a self-image without God only contains an empty promise—that success is attainable within ourselves. Too often, even as Christians, we assume that our ability to be successful is dependent upon the maturity of our self-confidence. However, seeking to free ourselves from a lack of self-confidence is the ultimate in frustration because it is truly unattainable.

Moses is not the only one who suffered with doubts about himself. King David experienced moments of uncertainty as he led the nation of Israel . . . Job also in his ordeal with physical pain . . . and the apostles as they assumed the leadership role for the early church. We follow in their footsteps with the same desire to be great in the kingdom of God. But we, too, must recognize that when *we* are presented with a significant challenge, we will question at least for a moment our ability to perform the task. If our true worth and ability to be successful in life rests solely within ourselves, then what is the need for faith in God?

The spoiled adolescent has a very difficult time relinquishing enough of his own authority to allow his identity to be remolded by God. However, he is trapped because he cannot find lasting security within himself either. His self-will has gotten him into so much trouble with others that the fear of rejection is ever present in his mind. Yet, it is that same self-will that is preventing him from finding comfort through being submissive to God's will. Because of his frustration, he may surmise that one easy way out of his dilemma is to withdraw himself physically and emotionally. His self-concept has become so fragile that he is unwilling to risk it by any future social involvement. Fearing that he will lose what little self-esteem he has left, he begins to make decisions about his participation in the world based upon whether or not he can avoid feelings of insecurity. As you know, there are very few situations in life where we are protected from such a possibility. However, his ego has become so sensitive that if someone attempts to give him constructive criticism or expresses a different opinion than his, he withdraws like a wounded animal.

He begins to realize that these are not like the old days when *he* was in control. People no longer agree with everything he does or says. Since he feels incapable of adapting to his new and threatening environment, he may choose a life of seclusion. In his search for self-worth, he concludes that a life of isolation will eliminate his feelings of insecurity. Unfortunately, he is mistaken. His unwillingness to socialize with others only causes his life to be controlled by fear— fear of failure and interpersonal relationships.

One of the ways that children manifest their fears is through withdrawal. But keep in mind that just because a child is withdrawn does not necessarily indicate that he is a spoiled and overprotected child. Such a lack of sensitivity and rash assessment of his character could bring about harmful consequences for years to come. There are a number of severe emotional disorders that have symptoms which are similar, one of the most common being acute depression.

This misdiagnosis had been made by a family I knew a few years ago. Cindy was the family member who initially came to me for help, and was the sister of a thirty-year-old man who still lived at home with his mom and dad. Although Cindy had left home and had been married for ten years, her brother's behavior continued to cause her great concern. Jeff had never held a job, and it appeared that he was a very self-centered person. Those who were unfamiliar with his life-style could not understand why his parents were constantly giving in to him. Their perception that his parents were permissive was merely an assumption, however, because few of them had even seen Jeff, let alone spoken with him. Even his close relatives believed that he was a spoiled brat—but little did they realize the seriousness of the young man's condition.

Jeff slept all day, coming down from his bedroom at night when it was time to eat supper with his mother and father, and only under the condition that no one else be present. One evening, while Jeff and his folks were eating dinner, friends of his parents decided to visit unannounced. As they approached the front porch of the home, their footsteps revealed their presence. Jeff, who became startled at the sound of strangers outside, quickly stopped eating and ran up the stairs to the security of his room, leaving his parents to explain that he was not feeling well.

Cindy shared with me that her brother had not bathed in over six months—neither had he shaved or changed his cloths. Jeff's disheveled appearance should have been a clue to those who loved him that he had a serious emotional illness. But to the untrained eye it appeared that he was just being a lazy bum. Based upon what was perceived to be his character, the young man's parents were encouraged to do everything from kicking him out of the house to protecting their son from the cruelty of the outside world. Responding to either one of these opposite ends of the spectrum would not provide the help that Jeff so desperately needed. Yet because his parents feared that any confrontation would cause him to become worse, they permitted his life of isolation to continue.

Friends and relatives were in disbelief, and asked why Jeff's mother and father would make such a decision. It was their opinion that if his mom and dad would only take a "hard line against his selfishness" that he would straighten up and become a responsible human being. Their opinions and suggestions, however, were based upon the false conclusion that his overdependence upon his parents was the reflection of a self-indulging, spoiled person. Fortunately for Jeff, his sister Cindy adopted a more balanced perspective of how he could be helped, realizing that neither her parent's fear nor the insensitivity of others would stimulate the help that Jeff needed.

Jeff should have received immediate medical, psychological and spiritual help, and in this regard, his parent's unwillingness to do so was indeed a form of overprotecting him. His withdrawal, in combination with other symptoms, clearly demonstrated that he was a very depressed young man. However, in his case, it was wrong to conclude that because his fears were manifested through withdrawal that it was simply the result of a spoiled nature. The unwillingness on the part of some family and friends to recognize the true nature of his problems hindered Jeff from receiving the care that he rightfully deserved and desperately needed.

It is not uncommon for the fear of failure during childhood or adolescence to stimulate a life of seclusion. When Jeff was a child, his lack of socialization was a sign of depression, but this is not always the case. Some children attempt to search for self-worth by manipulating their parents through *intentionally* withdrawing from their environment.

The spoiled adolescent is prone to this type of behavior more than others, and to understand why, we must go back and look at how he has related to people. He has grown accustomed to depending upon others, using his demanding nature to meet his own needs. But he has since learned that he cannot do this forever, and that his selfishness has only caused people to reject him. Because of this, loneliness becomes a key element of his life. We who have experienced feelings of emptiness realize how hasty a person can become in their desire to fill this void. Sometimes we get so desperate for love that we will withdraw from people if we know that it will draw attention to ourselves. This attention-getting mechanism is very powerful, and as ridiculous as it may appear, it is our misguided attempt to search for self-worth through making people feel sorry for us. This form of exploiting the love of friends and family can become ingrained within a child's character, and if it does, it will only intensify his feelings of rejection and low self-esteem.

This is not to say that every child who is shy or withdrawn has adopted this life-style on purpose just to get his own way. Whether or not his behavior is purposeful or by accident, it most often reflects a low self-esteem, and those of us who see a child acting this way must be careful in how we respond to him. If we, in our loving attempt to make the overprotected child feel better about himself, miscommunicate our love so that he believes we feel sorry for him, then he will use this opportunity to tug upon our heartstrings of sympathy, tempting us to jump in and take full responsibility for his life. This is the last thing he needs, however, because it will only intensify the dependent relationship that exists between him and those who are overprotecting him. Once again, he will be in the captain's chair, and we will become the galley slaves, for he has just found an alternative to a demanding nature. Realizing that in giving ultimatums he no longer maintains his position of control, he could begin to use withdrawal as a new method of expressing his self-centeredness. With this in mind, the spoiled adolescent can adopt this appearance of helplessness as a plea to make us believe that he is incapable of assuming responsibility for his life.

His insistence that we comply with this game of manipulation is dangerous because, first of all, he is not an invalid. Secondly, and most importantly, it encourages a never-ending, downward spiral of his self-esteem. Relationships that are established or nurtured on this basis have at their very heart a spirit of dishonesty, and as tough as this concept may be to swallow, self-worth will never survive in such an atmosphere. Essentially, what the spoiled adolescent says (although he may never really verbalize it) is, "If you love me, you will grant me the freedom to live my way." But this statement is inaccurate because how in the world can we entrust ourselves to a person who manipulates others for his own selfish purposes? In light of his scheme, he has failed to understand the proper role that truthfulness and trust play in establishing love between human beings. *Truth* in a relationship is validated not only by the accuracy of words spoken, but with a sincerity of one's character or actions as well. Truth is the hallowed ground upon which all successful relationships rest and, be it with God or man, the absence of this quality will undermine any loving relationship. *Trust* relies upon *truth* in order to exist. Trust is best exemplified in a willingness to place ourselves in the care of another with the confidence that we will not be used or betrayed. Simply put, trust *is* truth expressed in a loving relationship over time.

This concept escapes the thinking of the spoiled child. He fails to understand that his integrity and ultimately his self-esteem are dependent upon being truthful with others in order to reach full maturity. When he asks others to grant him freedom to live life his way, it is always at the expense of someone else, and he is shocked when he is rejected as a result. Most people are unwilling to relate with others on this basis. So with this in mind, we have now come full circle—the absence of truth destroys trust within a relationship, which erodes love, which culminates in rejection and a low self-esteem.

God is fully aware of the tragic consequence of dishonesty; therefore, He is truthful with us about who we are and how we can reach maturity in Him. Since He speaks the truth in love, we feel secure and entrust ourselves to Him, realizing that He has no deceitful motives. Likewise, He calls us to be straightforward with our children. With love as our goal, I would strongly suggest that we foil any attempts on the part of our kids when they communicate in an untruthful manner, whether it be in words or actions. Trust depends upon it, and love cannot survive without it.

Because the spoiled adolescent attempts to sidestep the truth of his own nature, he modifies his life-style to compensate for the insecurity within him. As we have discussed, he may search for self-worth by choosing the life of a chameleon, securing his self-esteem from the opinions of the world, withdrawing out of fear or giving an appearance of helplessness. No matter which choice he makes, he will learn that all of them are incapable of providing the self-esteem for which he is searching. Despite this fact, his selfish will remains undaunted because he knows that there is yet another avenue by which he can search for self-worth—jealousy.

When we think of jealousy, we usually think of it as an emotion or state of mind. However, this is not always the case because once this feeling becomes impassioned within us, it begins to manifest itself in our behavior toward others. Jealousy is a realized or a perceived threat of loss, and to fully understand this concept, we must recognize that jealousy centers itself around either loss of someone or something or feelings of inferiority. This is the emotion that you would most likely experience if someone stepped in and stole the heart of the one you loved. Likewise, you would feel the same way if, as you were growing up, someone that you loved and respected compared your appearance to that of your brother or sister or the child who lived next door. Maybe you were too tall, too short, skinny, fat, or had pimples or big feet. Throughout your adolescence, you may not have had the hairy chest like the other guy in gym class, or perhaps you had to wear a size "B" bra when the girl with the locker next to yours was wearing one much larger. If you experienced these feelings of inadequacy within your childhood, do you remember how you responded? If you were like most children, you immediately thought how much more recognition the other kid was getting, the one who was supposedly normal or more attractive. But ultimately, it was not the lack of notoriety that caused you to feel inferior, it was the fact that you presumably had less— less value, worth, and importance.

Jealousy is the natural outcome when we are threatened with the loss of love or worth. All of us have experienced this emotion, but the spoiled adolescent has not only *experienced* it, he attempts to *use* it to erase his deep sense of inferiority. Feeling threatened by not getting the attention or love he believes he deserves, he can pit friends and family members against one another. Ironically, his jealous emotions promote dissension and turmoil in the lives of those who love him the very most. Undermining their relationships is not without purpose, however, because it serves as a magnet for drawing attention to himself. By promoting hostility, he knows full well that all eyes will be pointed in his direction, giving him a tremendous feeling of power and self-importance. In a bizarre sort of way, he believes he has searched for and found self-worth through becoming the focus of everyone's attention. Little does he realize that this method of using jealousy to compensate for a low self-esteem will serve as the basis for his own downfall. Instead of compensating for feelings of loss and inferiority, he has actually brought the wrath of everyone upon himself. Yes, by creating chaos, he may revel in controlling his environment for a short while. But those around him will soon become wise to his little game, and he will receive exactly the opposite of what he wanted—rejection.

I surely do not want to appear as if I condone this method of responding to one who acts so foolishly. But neither do I want to paint a rosy picture in which everyone who associates with a boy or girl of this nature is going to automatically react with love and sensitivity. As a family counselor, I often speak with those who must live with such a teenager. I am convinced that they feel as though they are caught in a bind. No matter which way they turn, they experience an overwhelming sense of being trapped. On the one hand, it seems to them that overindulging the spoiled teenager only catapults him into a greater level of self-centeredness. Yet on the other hand, ignoring or rejecting him and leaving him to his own devices just perpetuates his loneliness and low self-esteem. Their feelings truly reflect the level of desperation within them, for in their opinion, they have run out of options to discipline him. It is not that these parents or grandparents are uncaring. It is just that they have lost their sympathetic chord. Their patience is growing fragile and thin because their household is in surrender to the spoiled adolescent's will.

---

[1] Taken from *The Sensation of Being Somebody*, by Maurice E. Wagner, Copyright 1975 by Maurice E. Wagner. Used by permission of Zondervan Publishing House.

[2] Taken from *Building Self-Esteem in the Family*. © 1977 Norman Wakefield, used with permission from David C. Cook Publishing Company.

6

Roadblocks
to Recovery

AS THE OVERPROTECTED CHILD finds himself fully involved in his adolescent years of life, his mother and father have before them the last opportunity to redirect his character. Only a precious few years remain to alter the course of how he is disciplined, for by the time their child becomes fifteen or sixteen years old, he will find it very difficult to escape the grip of his sheltered upbringing. Regardless of who may have overprotected their child—be it someone within the immediate family, grandparents, or another close relative—it is Mom and Dad who stand at a fork in the road. They can move in one of two directions: choosing to continue in the status quo, or deciding in favor of a higher standard of discipline. If they choose the latter, they should prepare themselves to hold on tight, because in doing so they will be confronted with a set of emotions and behaviors that can be very unsettling.

Little Johnnie is little no longer. He now stands eye to

eye with his parents, and their commitment to free him of his permissive past will be met with a flurry of resistance. His rebellion should not come as a surprise because, after all, he has grown accustomed to being in control. However, once his parents challenge his permissive environment to regain control of his life, he will feel threatened, for his sphere of influence is diminishing. He realizes that he will no longer be able to exercise his selfish, spoiled nature with impunity. The days when he was enabled with a strong base of authority are over, or so his parents would like to believe. Although they are committed to changing his behavior, their attempts to recover from his long reign of control will be very difficult. Years of frustration may have created emotional roadblocks which will prevent them from implementing what needs to be done.

Parents in our culture have to cope with tremendous burdens when it comes to raising their children. Everyone seems to be taking potshots at them to get them to make the "right" decisions, from the kind of cereal they should put in their kid's mouths to the methods of discipline they should employ. Moms and dads are pressed from every side as to what level of leadership they should exert in the correction of their children, and it is no wonder that many times they feel confused while swimming in a sea of apparently contradictory information. It is ironic, in light of all the help available to them, that they sometimes respond with a sense of *helplessness* which obstructs them from correcting their children at all.

One of the major causes of their feelings of helplessness can be traced to their fear of not wanting to make a mistake. None of us relish the thought of being viewed as an inadequate parent; thus, we do everything we can to insure that we operate at peak efficiency. However, in our zeal to become a superparent, we too often allow ourselves to be tossed to and fro by every opinion carried in the wind. As a result, we may never come to a firm conclusion upon whose opinions we will trust as we strive to become the very best parent.

With this in mind, let me incur the criticism of some of my professional colleagues by strongly suggesting that we rely upon the Lord as the ultimate authority in our leadership role over our children. In saying this, I am not suggesting that we turn a deaf ear to *godly wisdom* communicated to us through spiritual men and women. Such a claim would be indefensible, for this is one of the Lord's primary ways of helping us achieve His will (Proverbs 11:14). Neither am I trying to promote a philosophy of hiding our heads in the sand by ignoring the importance of a good education and being well-read. We should take advantage of every tool at our disposal in our goal to become loving disciplinarians. However, it goes without saying that the opinions expressed to us, regardless of the source, are only valid insofar as they submit to *His* book.

I was confronted with this issue very early in my graduate education. Institutes of higher learning are the graveyards of many a young Christian intending to enter the field of Marriage and Family Counseling. Those of us who decide upon this profession are bombarded with a myriad of philosophies as to how we can rid mankind of all his ills. Bucking the system can be costly, for anyone aspiring a Christian point of view will incur the rejection of most of his fellow students. This was illustrated during my Master's program when one of my clinical professors decided to share a *biblical* model of understanding human nature. Though the students were as polite as possible, one could not miss the chuckles, snickering comments, and sighs of disbelief. Their response was pale in comparison to the statements made after class was dismissed. "I can't believe that a man of his education can be so naïve," remarked one of his students. "Where did they (the administration) get this religious fanatic?" scoffed another.

You can imagine the pressure I was under to keep my

mouth shut. At that moment, I was confronted with a choice. Should I adopt the beliefs of everyone else and go along with the herd, or side with my professor and what the Lord had to say? Though I knew full well that the skeptics would look in my direction, I chose to embrace God's principles.

I realize in saying this that some could accuse me of espousing a narrow and pious point of view. This would be unfortunate because I am not suggesting a holier-than-thou attitude. What is at issue, however, is the inescapable fact that *all* of us, in varying degrees, depend upon others in formulating our beliefs. Whether this comes from a neighbor, our spouse, a philosophical thought, or the Lord, we will eventually be influenced to draw conclusions from them about ourselves, and yes, even about the way we raise our children. In graduate school, I decided to interpret my psychology in light of the Word of God, and not the reverse. In our homes, we will interpret our role as a mother and father by someone else's standard as well.

As parents, we find ourselves in the same arena as my professor, for there are some people within our society who strongly disagree (which is surely their right) with the Judeo-Christian values we espouse in the discipline of our children. Like my instructor, we too will risk the rejection of others as we follow in His will, and we should not become paralyzed in our parental leadership by attempting to please everybody. We are the guardians of our children's souls, and there is no need to feel helpless, or to apologize to anyone, in deciding to raise our children in the love and admonition of God.

As I discussed in an earlier chapter, one of the characteristics of all children is their natural inclination to be self-centered. This is especially true in the life of the spoiled child. And in light of his behavior, he is likely to elicit a great deal of frustration and anger from those who must live with him. This emotion becomes prevalent in the lives of his family because of his "tyranny." It is a human emotion and it is how people usually react when they realize that they may have been used, controlled, or manipulated for someone's selfish purposes. What I have just stated may sound rather harsh, but recall with me for a moment the last time someone took advantage of you. If you are like most people, you probably became angry. Reacting initially in this way may be in keeping with how you have been treated, but anger accumulated over several years turns into resentment, which presents a formidable roadblock in our desire to redirect the will of a child who has been overprotected and developed a spoiled nature.

The major confrontation we have to face in dealing with anger is a biblical one, and it would be a mistake to leap over Scripture in an attempt to resolve our emotions. Two passages of Scripture are of principal importance in this regard, the first being Ephesians 4:25–32:

> Therefore each of you must put off falsehood and speak truthfully to his neighbor, for we are all members of one body. "In your anger do not sin": Do not let the sun go down while you are still angry, and do not give the devil a foothold. He who has been stealing must steal no longer, but must work, doing something useful with his own hands, that he may have something to share with those in need. Do not let any unwholesome talk come out of your mouths, but only what is helpful for building others up according to their needs, that it may benefit those who listen. And do not grieve the Holy Spirit of God, with whom you were sealed for the day of redemption. Get rid of all bitterness, rage and anger, brawling and slander, along with every form of malice. Be kind and compassionate to one another, forgiving each other, just as in Christ God forgave you (NIV).

These words by the apostle Paul contain both an acknowledgement and a warning. First, he acknowledges that we can be within God's will and be angry at the same time. But his warning comes quickly on the heels of his preceding statement. He realizes that Christians, like everyone else, are quick to act upon their emotions.

This reminds me of a story about a group of eighteenth century Welsh coal miners. They were a rather tough and rowdy bunch whose ability to use profanity would embarrass even a crusty old fisherman. Most of their cursing was targeted at each other, but the packing mules which were used to haul the coal cars received a healthy dose of it as well. It's hard to know what the mules thought of all the salty language, but nevertheless, they responded when the miners gave them verbal commands in this way.

One summer an evangelist held a revival in their community, and with a little prodding from the ladies in town, the men reluctantly attended. To the surprise of most everyone except the preacher, a number of the miners committed their lives to Jesus Christ. As they began to learn more about God's will they also began to repent of their ways. Then, a very interesting phenomenon occurred—the efficiency of the mining operation dropped dramatically. This was highly unexpected because it was thought that the miners' newfound joy in Christ would only increase their productivity. But, upon further investigation, it was found that the work problem was related to the mules—they couldn't understand what the miners were saying anymore!

In reflecting upon his own past, Paul knew full well that the way we think and feel is logically reflected in our behavior. As we concentrate our thoughts upon God's values, our change in thinking should be clearly demonstrated through our behavior. But as you know, this is not always the case. Some people "push our button" and we lash out in anger. It is because of this that Paul proceeds to explain that stealing and verbal and physical abuse are among the by-products of any unresolved anger. Unfortunately, our mouths and hands too often become instruments of communicating how we truly feel.

With this in mind, we can see how anger makes its transition from biblical acceptance to sin as we make the transition from *feeling* angry to *becoming* resentful and retaliating. It is this issue of retaliation that some parents must tackle as they attempt to cope with an older child who has developed a spoiled nature.

Larry became the stepfather of such a child—a sixteen-year-old teenager to be exact. Larry was not aware of David's true nature until after he married the boy's mother. If only he had known what he was getting into. David had grown very accustomed to having his own way, which only intensified as he entered into adolescence. Despite his very bad grades, he already owned his own car and had all the gas and insurance his mom could buy. What a dynamite act! Although he had previously acknowledged a personal relationship with Christ, he lived by the old adage, "I love to sin, God loves to forgive—isn't this a splendid arrangement!" Well, his new stepfather wasn't at all pleased with this arrangement and decided to make amends for the years of overprotection by David's mother.

Despite the fact that he had failed to establish a friendship with David, Larry decided that a heavy-handed, authoritarian approach would make up for his step-son's irresponsibility. Like many teenagers David's mouth could test the patience of even the best parent, and Larry's frustration and anger had approached the tolerance limit. I asked Larry how he finally ended up confronting David about this lack of discipline, to which he answered, "I slugged him in the mouth!" As you can imagine, I was in sharp disagreement with his reply, so I asked him why he would do such a thing. Larry looked at me, and being fully convinced he said, "Because I wanted him to learn to respect me!"

Larry stepped over the line—the line between feeling angry and avenging himself—and it is no wonder that he failed to receive the respect that he desired from his new stepson. Instead of openly admitting that he was angry, and holding David accountable for his lack of discipline, Larry became resentful and redirected his feelings into a destructive act. Believing that he could make up for over a decade of permissiveness, Larry reacted in the *opposite* extreme, thereby transplanting his own resentfulness into David.

In light of Larry's behavior, our attention is drawn to the second Scripture verse pertaining to anger. It comes from James 1:19—20 which says:

> My dear brothers, take note of this: Everyone should be slow to speak, and slow to become angry, for man's anger does not bring about the righteous life which God desires (NIV).

If taken at face value, the two passages of Scripture which I have quoted could be interpreted as contradictory. On the other hand, Paul says that we can be angry, and yet James is saying that our anger will not culminate in godly living. Upon closer inspection, however, we begin to see that God has established a clear boundary for us to live by in our attempt to deal with anger—the boundary of retaliation.

At this juncture, parents who live with a teenager like David would find it very easy to draw a comparison between Larry's response and how they react to their own children. They might say to themselves that they have never taken revenge with physical abuse and are therefore well within the boundaries of God's will. However, we cannot absolve ourselves so quickly, because retaliation is not limited to just physical violence. It can become camouflaged in ways which are more socially acceptable. Not wanting to be like Larry, there are times when we suppress the resentment we have toward our children with the belief that it will somehow magically go away. We deny that its existence could be a stumbling block toward wholeness, so instead of forgiving each other before we go to bed, we side-step our anger by retiring it between the pages of sleep (Ephesians 4:26).

Responding to self-centered children by hiding resentfulness in a secret compartment of our heart only provides the seedbed for other types of retaliation such as gossip, the "silent treatment," and sarcasm. Sure, they may appear to be more "Christian," but these forms of punishment (which are much more prevalent than physical abuse) accomplish the same result—alienation from the ones we love.

We have just observed two roadblocks which hinder our recovery from resentfulness. First, through Larry's authoritarianism, which in his case was demonstrated through abusiveness, and secondly, the suppressing of one's emotions. Neither are worthy candidates to help parents in their recovery process toward redirecting the will of the spoiled child. This is due to the fact that both are extreme forms of "discipline." The first is a vain attempt to exert leadership and respect through the use of control. This only creates one battle after another and leaves love out of the process. The second appears to be more loving, but due to the element of withdrawal, it becomes a benign form of parental permission for their child to continue in his behavior. Each is incapable of making up for the years of overprotection and permissiveness because they fail to focus their attention upon the root causes of such styles of parenting.

7

Responding to the Surrendered Household

BEFORE WE BEGIN TO LOOK at the heart of what will change the nature of the overprotected and spoiled child, take a few moments to complete a short quiz from Dr. Dennis Guernsey about the four basic styles of parenting which we use in the raising of our children. Three of these styles can obstruct our efforts to respond to the child whose household is in surrender to his will. Please check the corresponding boxes of the statements that sound like what you might say to your children when they disagree, disobey, ask "why?", dawdle, make a mistake, and so forth. Think of your oldest child when you answer these questions. If you are yet to have children, think ahead. *Be honest!*

	YES	NO
1. You need your sleep . . . to bed, no arguments.	—	—

2. Rules are rules. You're late to dinner, so to bed with no supper.   ___   ___

3. You're late again to dinner, Tiger. How can we work this out?   ___   ___

4. Well, you can stay up this time . . . I know you like this program.   ___   ___

5. Work it out yourself . . . I'm busy.   ___   ___

6. I won't stand for your back talk. Apologize! (or *whack!*)   ___   ___

7. You can't get up because the kids wanted to stay out past ten o'clock? That's your problem . . . I've got to get to work.   ___   ___

8. Good grief! Can't you be more careful?   ___   ___

9. Hey, I wish I could let you stay up, but I don't feel good about you missing your sleep.   ___   ___

10. Late again, huh? Pass the meat, please.   ___   ___

11. When we both cool off, we better have a talk about this.   ___   ___

12. You're tired, aren't you? A paper route is a rough job . . . sure I'll take you around.   ___   ___

13. You didn't hear me call for dinner? Well, sit down . . . I don't want you eating cold food.   ___   ___

14. So you think I'm stupid, huh? That's your problem. Beat it.   ___   ___

15. You're really stuck, aren't you? Well, I'll bail you out this time and then let's figure a better way for the future.   ___   ___

16. Please don't be angry with me—you're making a scene.   ___   ___

17. I don't have to give you reasons. Just do as I say.   ___   ___

18. No son of mine is going to goof off. You
    took the job. You get it done.   ___   ___

19. You say all the other girls are going to the
    party? I'd like to have more information be-
    fore I say yes or no.   ___   ___

20. Jimmy, please try to hurry . . . Mommy will
    be late if we don't start soon.[1]   ___   ___

Before you turn to the appendix of the book for the
answers, lets' take a look at what these questions are trying
to measure. In Dr. Guernsey's research, his goal was to reveal what kind (styles) of parenting raise children who have
these four characteristics:

1. *High self-worth:* This means that children have a sense of
   self-respect and are happy to be who they are.
2. *Conform to the authority of others:* In other words, do
   children get along with such people as their teachers in
   school or church, their parents, and others in positions of
   authority?
3. *Follow the religious beliefs of their parents.*
4. *Identifying with the counterculture.* A counterculture
   runs opposite to what is accepted as right and good by
   the established culture. In one city the counterculture
   may be drug oriented, while another revolves around
   gangs, and so forth. It should be explained that some
   identification with the counterculture or rebelliousness is
   normal in the teen years. However, it becomes dangerous
   when the child's life-style and the well-being of the family unit becomes impaired.[2]

As Dr. Guernsey began to look at children who manifested these four characteristics, his research revealed that
there were two very powerful factors related to parents that
influenced their sons and daughters to become this way:
parental control, the ability of a parent to manage his child's

behavior, and *parental support,* the ability to make the child feel loved.

As you look at the following page entitled "Styles of Parenting"[3] you will notice that the balance of *support* versus *control* can influence greatly the degree to which children adopt or reject the four characteristics of high self-worth, conforming to authority, following in their parents' religious beliefs, and identification with the counterculture. We will begin first by looking at the *authoritarian* style of parenting in the bottom right corner. Remember that #1 indicates a high level and is the most desirable score—except in the fourth characteristic, identification with the counterculture.

Authoritarian

The authoritarian parent is a high control, low support parent. He has high expectations for the management of his child's behavior; however, his child has a difficult time feeling as if he is loved. Based upon the findings of the research, children of authoritarian parents scored third or next to the last in a positive self-worth. Likewise, they ranked last in conforming to the authority of others and following in the religious beliefs of their parents. They tied for first in identifying with the counterculture.

Neglectful

Parents were thought to have a neglectful style of parenting when they showed little ability to either make their child feel loved or control his behavior. The research indicated that their children had the lowest self-esteem (#4), were virtually last in conforming to authority and following in the religious beliefs of their parents. They tied with children from authoritarian parents in identifying with the counterculture the most.

Permissive

As I stated earlier in the book, permissive parents really know how to make their children feel loved. Yet they

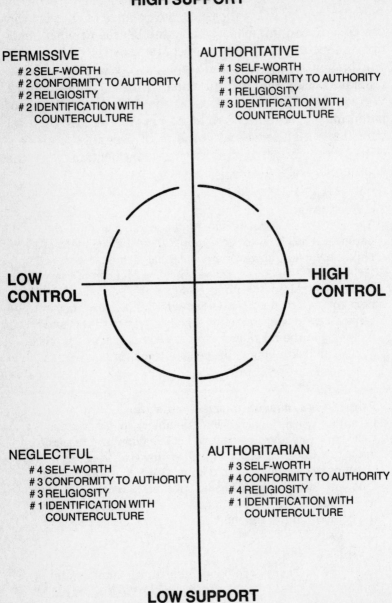

STYLES OF PARENTING
HIGH SUPPORT

PERMISSIVE
- # 2 SELF-WORTH
- # 2 CONFORMITY TO AUTHORITY
- # 2 RELIGIOSITY
- # 2 IDENTIFICATION WITH
    COUNTERCULTURE

AUTHORITATIVE
- # 1 SELF-WORTH
- # 1 CONFORMITY TO AUTHORITY
- # 1 RELIGIOSITY
- # 3 IDENTIFICATION WITH
    COUNTERCULTURE

LOW CONTROL

HIGH CONTROL

NEGLECTFUL
- # 4 SELF-WORTH
- # 3 CONFORMITY TO AUTHORITY
- # 3 RELIGIOSITY
- # 1 IDENTIFICATION WITH
    COUNTERCULTURE

AUTHORITARIAN
- # 3 SELF-WORTH
- # 4 CONFORMITY TO AUTHORITY
- # 4 RELIGIOSITY
- # 1 IDENTIFICATION WITH
    COUNTERCULTURE

LOW SUPPORT

become easily exasperated in managing their child's behavior. Therefore, their *child* is in control of the home. Generally, children from these parents score second best in self-worth, conforming to authority, and following in their parent's religious beliefs. Despite all of these positive qualities, however, permissive parents raise children who rank almost at the top in identifying with the counterculture.

Authoritative
Authoritative parents demonstrate consistently an ability to *manage* their child's behavior, and in combination with their ability to communicate love, their son or daughter views them as *leaders* to be followed. Because of this, their children score the highest in conforming to their authority, as well as following in their parent's religious footsteps. Also they score last in identification with the counterculture.

The results of this research have tremendous implications for all parents, especially to those who have lived with an overprotected child. It would be easy to conclude that the best way to counteract overprotection and permissiveness is to head in the opposite direction. Logic may also reinforce this thought. However, the best way to compensate for a lack of discipline will not be accomplished through its antithesis—authoritarianism.

If we were to adopt this style of parenting as a prescription for the ills of permissiveness, it would be tantamount to a physician telling his middle-aged, overweight, and under-exercised patient to immediately stop eating and run ten miles everyday. Despite the fact that it is impractical, it won't work. Furthermore, this advice would cause serious health problems, and in some cases possibly even death. Therefore, an authoritarian approach to parenting fails in it's attempt to pry control out of the hands of the overprotected and spoiled child because it neglects to communicate love in the process, usually culminating in the demise of the parent-child relationship as well.

Since this is the case, why does the research indicate that a number of children from authoritarian homes choose to become involved in the counterculture? It doesn't make sense that a child with a high-control parent would rebel against that control only to join up with a gang or other group where the element of control—and consequences for actions—is far greater that that of the home from which they came!

There is only one answer that seems plausible, and it evolves around the issue of love and belonging. On the surface, it appears to be a twisted form of reasoning, but nevertheless, the counterculture provides the boost in self-esteem for which many adolescents are starving. Despite the reality that their rebelliousness could cost them their lives, teenagers are more than willing to submit to the authority of a gang or another subculture. And for what? Because they feel loved and respected. As a result, they experience a sense of worth and purpose. Surely, I am not suggesting that we supplement our young people's self-esteem by encouraging them to rebel against parental authority in favor of joining a gang or another malevolent group. However, the lesson is clear. Parents who expect obedience but neglect to balance that with an equal amount of supporting love run a substantial risk of having their children lured into an element of society that *will* give them that love.

So, how can we prevent or reverse this trend in a child who is being overprotected and developing a spoiled nature? Walking the road of permissiveness or authoritarianism cannot help us achieve this goal. Therefore, what are the ingredients necessary to communicate love's delicate balance of support and discipline so our children can become emancipated, having been fully equipped to successfully confront the trials and demands of life?

Unconditional Love Contains the Freedom to Fail

Few of us will ever forget the 1984 Summer Olympic Games held in Los Angeles, California. This was especially true of those who lived in the immediate area. I watched alongside my relatives as the Olympic torch passed in front of my family's home, and we, like most of the nation, were held captive by the games for over two weeks. There are several memorable moments which I have stored away on video tape, but the event which I will forever remember was the women's marathon.

Those who are sports aficionados will recall that it was American runner Joan Benoit who won the gold medal. She ran the third fastest woman's marathon in history, completely outclassing the field of runners. Yet it was a thirty-nine-year-old Swiss-American named Gabriella Anderson-Scheiss who captured the hearts of many that day. Running for her native country, she had completed 25.5 miles of the race, and less than a half mile from the finish line, something extraordinary happened. Just as she was to enter the long tunnel leading to the coliseum floor, her mind decided that it had had enough. Despite her years of experience and training, the race which started at Santa Monica college finally took its toll. Gabriella was on the verge of heatstroke, and her body temperature was approaching the dangerously high temperature of 106 degrees.

As she entered the coliseum, one could have mistaken her to be intoxicated. She had a glazed stare upon her face, and her body was weaving like that of a toddler on new-found legs. Step after step, it appeared to the 100,000 people in attendance that she was out of control. The final lap around the track must have been the longest 500 meters in her life. Unable to run any further, she was now walking, or so it appeared. Back and forth across the lane lines she plodded along her jagged course, her left arm swinging limply. It was a pitiful sight. Although she could no longer walk in a straight path, she still had the presence of mind to focus her attention on the finish line. She had trained all of her life for this day, and since this was her last opportunity to run in the Olympics, she would not allow this chance of a lifetime to be taken from her.

During the final minutes of her ordeal, many people called for someone to intervene and remove her from the track. Television and radio commentators criticized those closest to Gabriella for not forcing her to leave. Her agony must have been especially painful for her husband and coach as they watched their loved one pushing herself to the outer limits of endurance. They were as vitally concerned about her health as anyone, yet they knew her very well. They had trained alongside her throughout the years, and better than anyone, they could gauge the fine line that separated possible injury from her success.

The writer of Hebrews shares with us words that are of special importance:

> Therefore, since we are surrounded by so great a cloud of witnesses, let us also lay aside every weight, and sin which clings so closely, and let us run with perseverance the race that is set before us, looking to Jesus the pioneer and perfecter of our faith . . . (12:1–2).

Without a doubt, raising children is the ultimate endurance race. During this marathon event, their family, especially their parents, are the "cloud of witnesses" observing their every move. In light of Gabriella's condition it would have been easy, and some would say loving, for her family to jump out of the stands and sweep her to safety. Parents face the same temptation every time their children make a mistake or appear to be in trouble. And it is at the time when children struggle that Mom and Dad are the most vulnerable in this regard. They are being torn in opposite directions. Should they step in and help their child, or should they not?

This tension is ever present within them because they are being pulled by two very powerful, and opposing forces—*their* desire to be a loving parent by being available whenever their child needs them and their *children's* need to build self-confidence by developing the skills to overcome trials on their own.

Thus, the key to a parent's success as to whether to jump in or stay out of it lies not only in the training they put their children through, but in *letting them run the race*! As in the case of Gabriella Anderson-Scheiss, her family was involved daily in her training. As a result, they were intimately aware of her tolerance limits. They knew what she was equipped to handle. But all of her knowledge and preparation would have been wasted if she had been restrained from stepping on the track, or removed from it, for fear of her stumbling or failure. They gave her the freedom to fail. Likewise, it is the same for us as we watch our children run the race of life. In light of this, we now approach *the* most difficult issue within this book, and unless we can conquer it, the grip of overprotection will maintain its hold upon us.

Discipline Is Painful

"My son, do not regard lightly the discipline of the Lord, nor lose courage when you are punished by him. For the Lord disciplines him whom he loves, and chastises every son whom he receives." It is for discipline that you have to endure. God is treating you as sons; for what son is there whom his father does not discipline? If you are left without discipline, in which all have participated, then you are illegitimate children and not sons. Besides this, we have had earthly fathers to discipline us and we respected them. Shall we not much more be subject to the Father of spirits and live? For they disciplined us for a short time at their pleasure, but he disciplines us for our good, that we may share his holiness. *For the moment all discipline seems painful rather than pleasant; later it yields the peaceful fruit of righteousness to those who are trained by it.* Therefore, lift your drooping hands and strengthen your weak knees, and make straight paths for your feet, so that what is lame may not be put out of joint but rather be healed (Hebrews 12:5–13, italics mine).

Pain is a four-letter word! Usually, it is unspeakable within the context of child discipline, and for parents, it is hard to associate this word within the framework of a loving, parent-child relationship. Love and pain . . . together they seem out of place. Yet, there are few worthwhile pursuits in life that are devoid of pain, and this is especially true in the training of children. Despite this, however, the relationship that pain has with the correcting of children may be anathema because it immediately conjures up issues associated with abuse. Therefore, in context with the true issue at hand, let me leave no room for doubt. *Pain, as it relates to discipline, is not a license for the mistreatment of our children.*

In discussing this issue of how discipline is painful, I am not going to focus our attention so much on the spanking of children. Although it is many times over-used, physical discipline, when applied appropriately, is an effective and biblical method of correcting children. To study that concept more closely, I would suggest that you read Dr. James Dobson's book entitled, *Dare to Discipline.* What I am drawing our attention to, however, is pain's impact upon our children's emotional growth and development.

Pain is a necessary fact of life. To deny its existence not only colors reality, but sets up a chain of events that will incapacitate our children from becoming successful. Our goal is not to create a life of pain, but rather to equip them with the tools to conquer it. This occurs initially by teaching them a healthy respect for it. We don't give our children permission to run across streets, play with sharp instruments, or accept rides from strangers. Neither do we allow them to take out their frustrations by hurting others. However, this equipping process cannot stop with simply the physical dimension of pain, for the emotional dimension is just as vital.

Parents do not like to see their children suffer. Our little ones realize from their earliest days of life that comfort and security is found within the arms of their mother and father. They recognize that Mom and Dad are quick to respond whenever they become frightened. This initial stage of dependency and bonding is very important to cultivate because their physical and emotional survival rest upon it. We need to communicate our willingness to be sensitive to our children's fears. Beyond this level of tenderness, however, there are some parents and/or family members who will do everything they can to *eliminate* emotional discomfort from their children's lives. If they erect such a barrier to ward off all pain, then their son or daughter will conclude that he or she will be rescued every time it raises its ugly head.

This is, of course, an unrealistic expectation. As a child progresses down the road toward adulthood, his parents will not always be there every time he hurts himself, is rejected by one of his peers, or feels lonely. His folks will not live forever.

Nevertheless, with his false expectation in tow, he may begin to build a self-destructive form of dependency . . . through coping with emotional pain by drawing closer and closer to the one who is sheltering him. He is not becoming equipped to confront his fears because others are protecting him from them. As a result, he is being robbed of the opportunity to build self-confidence through overcoming life's difficulties with his *own* God-given abilities. He has concluded that others believe he can't do it! Therefore, in our loving attempt to *eliminate* fear from his life, he lacks coping skills, which *creates* fear instead. And fear only increases his inability to cope with problems.

Children who are overprotected in this manner grow up to feel like losers. They recoil from opportunities for success. As they strive to achieve, they lack the perseverance required to plow through the pain and insecurity that comes with success. With this in mind, it is imperative that parents not get overly concerned when their children express signs of fear, for if they do so, little Johnnie or Susie may perceive that Mom and Dad are afraid and therefore become even more insecure and fearful.

Several months ago I was speaking with the mother of a six-year-old boy. Every parent would love to have a son like him—he was at the top of his class, socialized well with his peers, and was easy to discipline. When he was about to enter the second grade, however, his best friend moved to another neighborhood. Soon after this, he became afraid and cried each morning before he was to leave on the bus for school. Mom thought his behavior to be very uncharacteristic, so she began to inquire of his teachers how he was doing otherwise. Everyone was in agreement—after several minutes of crying, he calmed down and became his happy, normal self. With his mother's encouragement that he was going to be all right, and by taking him to school herself, his crying spells began to diminish after a few days.

Surprisingly, however, her son regressed after several weeks. As his mother and I discussed the situation, it became evident he was doing so because she was giving him mixed messages. In her attempt to help him overcome the insecurity surrounding the loss of his friend, she undermined her efforts by paying considerable attention to him every time he cried. Furthermore, she would no longer permit him to ride the bus to school, which confused him even more. He said to himself, "If I'm going to be O.K., then why is my mother hovering over me?"

Her son was very perceptive. Why did these loving responses on her part backfire? Initially, because she followed through with her sensitivity for too long after the first signs of his insecurity. Beyond that, however, Mom was unaware that there is a distinct difference between *paying attention* and *observing* her child's fears. Unless there is a clear and compelling reason to do so, too much attention focused on a child's insecurity causes him to erroneously conclude that

Mom and Dad are afraid as well. In light of this, it is without question that we need to keep a close eye on our children when they become troubled or worried, but not to such an extent that we exacerbate their insecurity.

For most of us, we begin to see the signs of fear in children very quickly—even as soon as the first few years of life. They appear emotionally immature and find social interaction with their peers very difficult. As a result, they may be described as "clingy." Some insecurity in this regard is normal, especially during the period of separation anxiety centered around nine to eighteen months of age. However, fear with the overprotected child is not limited to a brief period of his life. Rather, he manifests a *demeanor of fear* well into his grade school years, which serves beautifully as a means to draw attention and cause others to hover over him. Sheltering him in this way only reinforces his thought that there is something to be afraid of. Like the Cowardly Lion in the *Wizard of Oz*, his greatest wish will be that of courage.

Our children cannot build self-confidence and solve life's difficulties if they are afraid of their world. Fear does not equip them with the ability to cope with the problems— it only diminishes it. Therefore, we need to build within them the courage to overcome this and other kinds of emotional pain. In light of this, let me make the following suggestion . . . that we help our children cope with pain by exposing them to it. That is, let's inoculate them against what could be the paralyzing effects of pain by permitting them to experience a small amount of it.

At first, this suggestion might seem beyond the bounds of reason, because after all, we don't apply *hot* compresses to cure a high fever, and neither do we give a cup of water to a drowning man. However, modern medicine routinely uses the principle which I have just suggested to cure several major illnesses.

Some of you may remember pictures of hospital wards lined with rows of "iron lungs." This was an all-too-familiar sight from 1915 through 1954 because it represented the crippling effects of the poliomyelitis virus. The initial symptoms of this disease seemed innocent enough—a headache, sore throat and fever—somewhat like a bad cold. However, in some cases it was followed by pain in the neck and back muscles, and in severe cases, by muscular weakness and possibly paralysis. Sixty thousand people died! It is no wonder that parents became alarmed when they observed these symptoms in their children, for this is not what they would have expected during the summer—the dreaded "polio season."

Watching thousands of children gasp for air in a desperate struggle to breathe has a way of mobilizing the medical community to find a cure very quickly. Hundreds of physicians and scientists were involved in the project, and it wasn't until a little-known researcher named Jonas Salk peered through his microscope that a cure was found. Imagine his elation at the very moment of his discovery. Like the old miner who after years of hard work finally found his vein of gold, Dr. Salk probably yelled, "Eureka, I have found it!"

His colleagues must have been equally enthusiastic as they inquired of him how he made his discovery. "Well," said Dr. Salk, "I found that if you alter the polio virus just a little bit and then inject it into a person's body, they won't *acquire* the disease, they will be immunized against it!" To the medical community, the idea of a vaccine was not totally foreign. But imagine the skepticism and mockery he faced from friends, fearful parents, and the people in general. "Just think of it," they said, "Dr. Salk proposes that we *cure* polio by *giving* people polio!"

Since the Salk vaccine, polio is a word used most often in passing conversations. This disease has been eliminated from most of the modern world, limited to a few outbreaks for those who have not been vaccinated against it. The laughter and skepticism has died down because the pain and suffering has stopped.

The medical community has taught us an extremely

valuable lesson—that you can prevent some diseases by exposing people to them. Likewise, we as parents hold the key to eliminating overprotection and the long-term, debilitating effects of emotional pain by allowing our children exposure to life's uncomfortable moments. This is very difficult for us to do, but we must give ourselves permission to inoculate them against the paralyzing effects of the harsh realities of this world.

Jesus modeled for us how this is done by the way in which He interacted with His apostles. Our Lord could have taken the Twelve, hid in the caves above the Sea of Galilee, and just taught them everything about life. But He did not. He knew they were to experience some very rough times together and that there was more to equipping the saints for the work of the ministry than merely instructing them. So it is in the equipping of our children. They need to be given the freedom to run the race and put into practice what we have taught them while not being overprotected from the possibility of failure. Yes, they will "blow it," stub their toes, and experience rejection, but once we have completed their godly training they will be successful in their pursuits.

At times, we will have to pick them up when they become insecure and frightened, and encourage them on their way. This begins as soon as our little "ankle biters" put that very first knot on their forehead, and continues until the day we watch them leave for college or join with another in marriage. We will be to them as the Holy Spirit is to us—a "comforter" (John 14:16)—one who comes alongside of to intercede or help on behalf of another. Despite our best intentions, however, the pain that is associated with discipline is just as much a reality for parents to live with as it is for their children.

Discipline is Not Defined by Our Emotions

You have heard the old saying, "This is going to hurt me more than it's going to hurt you." There is an element of truth in this, because another painful aspect of parenting is the fact that we will incur pain upon ourselves as well. Because this is true, one source of overprotecting and spoiling a child begins by protecting *ourselves* from the pain associated with discipline. There are times when we must be willing to experience some discomfort in order to obtain a better perspective of what is in our children's best interests.

One Saturday afternoon, our daughter Nicole developed one of her usual cravings for pizza. Since it was not uncommon for my wife and I to take the kids out to lunch, I began to pack up the family and head off to Chuck-E-Cheese's, the local pizza parlor. If the truth be known, giant stuffed animals dancing on stage to the tune of loud music is not always my idea of fun. Throw in forty or fifty wiggly pre-schoolers (all of whom border on hyperactive) and we were set for a "thrilling" afternoon. Despite the insanity, I really looked forward to going out with my family, and of course Nicole was ecstatic about the idea. As we prepared ourselves to leave, my wife Diane wondered what all of the excitement was about. So I went on to explain that ol' Dad had agreed to his daughter's request for lunch.

Based upon Diane's reaction, it took me only a moment to conclude that something was amiss. As Diane looked at Nicole, I began to realize that I had been caught in a power play of wills. My wife had already told our daughter that we could not go out to Chuck-E-Cheese's! Nicole understood that it was wrong to reach for a second opinion whenever she didn't get her way. And although she hadn't actually lied to us, she was deceitful nevertheless.

It was very difficult for me to look into my little girl's big blue eyes and retract my earlier agreement. Despite her pouting and tears, I knew that we could not submit to her request. This was emotionally painful for me, too, yet to allow my daughter to do as she wanted would have undermined my wife's authority and reinforced Nicole's belief that she could divide and conquer our leadership. I was as disappointed as she was because I receive great joy from having a good time with my children. Her need for discipline, however, could not be guided by my emotions. Although I had misgivings, I realized that her growth and maturity was dependent upon denying myself the privilege of giving to Nicole what I knew would please her. At that moment, my goal was to love her for what she needed to become—honest and truthful—although it was very uncomfortable for me.

Parents undergo emotional discomfort not only by withholding pleasurable experiences from their children, but also because their children are asking for more detailed information in order to cope with life. The older our kids become, the greater their potential for getting into trouble. When they speak that first word of profanity or ask a question related to sex, how do we respond? For some of us our initial reaction is one of shock, which is usually followed immediately by fear—fear of doing an inadequate job as a parent, fear of our son or daughter being corrupted by worldly values. Although our response is justifiable to some degree, this emotion can render us powerless to answer their questions. As a result, moms and dads must recognize that their own fears have the potential of extinguishing communication within the family system by causing them to withdraw, culminating in their children's overprotection.

This process occurs so subtly that many times it passes without being noticed. I remember the story of the very young boy who came home from his first day at school and sat down for supper with his family. After he gave the prayer, he looked to his father and said, "Please pass the damned potatoes!" His parents, taken by surprise and unprepared to discuss his language, became apprehensive and merely hustled him off to his bedroom for a spanking. After he had sufficiently recovered, he resumed eating with his family. The older brother, who was in obvious glee over his younger brother's misfortune, leaned over and said to him, "Well, did you learn your lesson?" To which the little boy replied, "Yeah I learned never again to ask for those damned potatoes!"

What went wrong here, and why did he fail to learn his lesson? First, we must recognize that the potential for parents to be bushwhacked by this type of behavior exists within every child, no matter what their upbringing. Beyond the obvious, however, the boy's mother and father were overcome by his conduct. Yes, their son experienced a spanking, but he didn't know why. Their lack of communication told him that they were afraid to discuss the matter, and as a result, a critical element of discipline was inadvertently overlooked—instruction. Their son's failure to learn was fueled by a lack of parental readiness to discuss the uncomfortable, which short-circuited the lines of communication necessary to equip him for the future.

At this moment, there may be some who feel uncomfortable about the fact that I just used the word "damned." Please don't be dismayed. I wouldn't condone its use by my own children and neither would I encourage it for yours. However, if this word, or obscenities, or issues such as sexuality, drugs, secular music, and so on are so emotionally unsettling to you that you retreat from discussing them with your children, then perhaps they believe you are unapproachable as well. Our society, on the other hand, is not so shy. The movie industry, print media, and commercial advertisers are more than willing to be first in line to bombard our kids with whatever will turn a profit, illicit or not. The days when our sons and daughters learned about such things from etchings on a bathroom wall are over.

In light of this, it is a futile effort to attempt to cover their ears or conceal their eyes from reality. Pulling down the window shades and eliminating television won't prevent them from confronting the inevitable of what is in the world around them. There are no hiding places, and sooner than we would like to admit, our children will be outside the bounds of our control. Therefore, our only real hope for their lasting protection is for Mom and Dad to stretch beyond their own level of discomfort and clothe their boys and girls with the tools to deal with such topics biblically and concretely. If we fail to rise above our own personal insecurities in discussing such delicate matters, we will be faced with the most disturbing alternative—that our children will be left to cope with the trials and temptations of this society on their own. We need to be ever mindful of this question, "Does keeping a child in a state of ignorance actually promote Christ-like behavior?" If our Lord were to have adapted this point of view, the Bible would have all the depth of the *National Enquirer.* God loves us too much to be so glib. He realizes that the answer to the above question is "no" because communicating the truth about our world in an atmosphere of love and acceptance is the key to *eliminating* sin in His children's lives.

There is, however, a continual temptation for us to shelter our own children from reality. It is because of this that a significant part of pre-adolescent and teenage rebellion is a reflection of their parent's desire to overprotect them. In failing to address those issues so critical to their maturity, spiritual growth takes a back seat to our level of emotional comfort, which promotes our sons and daughters to look for life's answers within themselves, through experimentation, or from others.

As a result, their respect for us is lost—that ingredient which is so crucial in equipping our young people to say "no" when the world lures them in the opposite direction. Giving them the facts is simply not enough. The apostle Paul said in 2 Timothy 3:16–17:

> All scripture is inspired by God and is profitable for teaching, for reproof, for correction, and for training in righteousness, that the man of God may be complete, equipped for every good work.

However, Paul maintained a warm and intimate relationship with those to whom he spoke, and frankly, our children are not really going to care how much we *know* until they know how much we *care.*

Discipline Risks Rejection

Shortly after the birth of our second daughter, Laura, my wife set out on a program to get back into shape. For some reason, probably because her muscles had been stretched beyond their capacity, she had become much larger than with our first child. Like most women, Diane was concerned about her appearance, and the fact that her belly-button had extended into a different time zone made her all the more dedicated to look her best after the delivery. Several weeks into her fitness program she was doing exceptionally well, and our first daughter, Nicky, decided to make a comment.

As any set of parents can attest, the first few weeks with a breast-fed newborn are maddening. The last thing a mother in this situation wants to hear, especially early in the morning, is a misplaced comment by her bright-eyed preschooler. The day had barely begun, and my wife was attempting to help Nicky get her clothes in order. Believing that Nicky was in the process of putting her clothes on, Diane stepped into our bedroom to dress herself. My wife, unaware that she had been followed, joyfully began to slip on her next size smaller pair of pants. As she was doing so, my daughter, who was watching her from behind, remarked, "Well, look at those fat buns!" To my surprise, my wife shrugged off the comment and went about her day in a joyful mood. With what I believed to be an affront against her character, Diane remained secure, laughing because she found Nicky's comment to be humorous. Something within my wife allowed her to respond with such poise.

It takes a parent with a strong sense of inner security to withstand comments such as these, because children, through their words and actions, can molest our self-esteem. Based upon from whom our worth is derived, remarks such as my daughter's can either be humorous or cause us to question our value as a human being. If we do not possess an adequate self-concept, or if we seek the reinforcement of our self-concept from the wrong sources, then it may cause us to overprotect our child and result in his undisciplined nature.

Without a doubt, our children contribute greatly toward our sense of accomplishment as parents. We receive tremendous emotional support from our kids, primarily by watching them grow up to reflect the nature of God through the love and discipline of their mom and dad. When they fall short of our expectations, however, we immediately look within ourselves and become insecure and question how *we* may have failed. This is unfortunate, because children are naturally undisciplined. Their disobedience may not reflect an inadequacy on the part of their mother and father at all. Nevertheless, our tendency is to link our sense of worth to how well our children behave. If we do so, *our* self-esteem becomes dependent upon how well-mannered *they* are, and this reverse dependency spells disaster for any parent-child relationship.

It is satisfying to know that our son or daughter likes who we are. This gives us a warm feeling inside; however, we are not in a popularity contest. I have seen too many mothers and fathers in my office who succumb to the pressure of feeling they were disapproved of by their son or daughter. I wonder what we should expect in that regard? Is it reasonable to believe that while we are in the throes of disciplining our children that they should rise up and call us blessed? I think not. If we carry this idea to its next logical extension, then in order to avoid conflict and have our egos damaged, we ought to seek ratification of our decisions from our children prior to implementing them. Nothing would create greater chaos.

I don't want to suggest that we should be insensitive toward their point of view, or that we should not work together with them in making certain decisions. Inviting our children to express their opinions helps build their self-esteem and communicates that we are not authoritarian but are sensitive to their input. Furthermore, this openness provides a model by which they can make mature decisions in their adult life. However, if we continually seek their approval as a way of building our own self-concept, then *we* will become dependent upon *them*. As a result, our discipline of them may suffer for fear of our child not liking us. For this reason, if we are to avoid this dilemma, we must see that there is a significant difference between being *approved* of by our children and being *respected* by them.

Those of us in the "helping professions" confront this issue on a daily basis. Regularly, we set aside what feels comfortable in order to help those who are struggling with personal or family problems. When an individual or couple seeks our professional advice to locate the cause of their difficulties, it would be easy for us to tell them what they want to hear and thereby insure their approval. Finding favor in their sight may feed our egos; however, our actions would be the epitome of unprofessional conduct. In our search to explore the source of their pain, we risk inflicting another type of pain: expressing to them something that they would rather not hear and becoming vulnerable to their rejection.

Three years ago, a very good friend of mine found a lump on the back of his shoulder. On the day of his exploratory surgery, I spent the entire morning with the family attemping to ease their anxious hearts as we awaited the diagnosis. As the doctor sat with us in the consultation room, I will never forget his words, "It is a very aggressive form of cancer." Within four months, just a few days before Christmas, my friend was dead.

I tried to place myself in the doctor's position as he shared the truth of what he had found. Though he expressed much love and concern, I could see the tension on his face even before he spoke, for he knew the pain his diagnosis would cause within the family. It would have been much easier upon us all if the doctor had said not to worry because our friend had a benign tumor, and his health would be restored quickly. If he had made such a ludicrous remark, it would have been nothing short of malpractice. Though we did not find comfort in what he said, we respected the physician for his honesty.

As parents, we are continually placed in the same position as that doctor. We are entrusted by God to take spiritual X-rays of our children's lives perceiving that which they fail to see within themselves. When we begin to recognize their rebellious nature, which threatens their spiritual and emotional life, we are placed in a very uncomfortable position—shall we ignore the truth, or be honest? If we need their approval in order to reinforce our self-worth, then we will be tempted to ignore the truth of their sinfulness. If we want their respect, then we must confront their disobedience. Choosing this latter course of action runs the risk of their rejection; however, in the long run, *we* will find security and self-satisfaction as we watch our children grow into the likeness of Jesus Christ.

---

[1] Taken from *What Kind of Parent Are You?* By Dr. Dennis Guernsey in Family Life Today, January 1975. Used by permission of Dr. Dennis Guernsey. Copyright by Gospel Light Publications, Glendale, California, 91204.

[2] Ibid.

[3] Ibid.

8

The Spoiled "Child" in Leadership

SOMEWHERE, SOMETIME, WE ARE going to meet this person. Our lives may have been already touched by him. Some of us may recognize him as a boss, a spouse, a minister, or the person who lives next door. Outwardly he appears very tough—a regular John Wayne—always in control of his life and determined to get ahead. But in reality, he is more like a clam—a hardened shell on the outside, yet on the inside, vulnerable and very tender. There is a child trapped within him, an inner child of his past . . . warm . . . sensitive . . . yearning to be transparent with his feelings. But he is also afraid—afraid of rejection and afraid of being loved. Often he rejects before he can be rejected.

He maintains his outer crust to ward off the possibility of being bruised emotionally. Like ghosts from the past, the shackles of self-centeredness and insecurity continue to burden him. You are never really sure where you stand with him because he is never really sure of himself. He often knows what he wants and may even know how to get there; however; a pile of broken relationships usually lay at the bottom of his aspirations. He is the overprotected child turned spoiled, who is now an adult and in a position of leadership.

The day started early, 5:00 a.m.—a normal time to awake for Doug's line of work. This morning was not like most because today was very special—he was to go on "parade." It was his very first "parade and review" marching before his commanding officers. No, he was not a basic army recruit; Doug was a drill sergeant leading his very first company of soldiers.

This was a unique opportunity for leadership, one that he had never experienced previously. Prior to this he had spent most of his time in the sheltered confines of an office, pushing paperwork and watching his superiors carry out the task he was about to perform. Although he had plenty of time in the service and the stripes to prove his authority, actual experience had eluded him.

Those of you with a history of military service are very familiar with the preparation that surrounds this event. It is the highlight of basic training. With shoes spit-shined and uniforms donned meticulously, this is the time for the soldiers to march in perfect columns—to strut their stuff and show what they know. This is the day when drill instructors have the possibility of *their* name being placed at the top of the list as the instructor with the best company of men in all of basic training.

The time had come and Doug's troops were ready. The reviewing stands were draped in red, white, and blue banners. Proud mothers and fathers, with cameras ready, anxiously anticipated the start of the parade. And so it did. Thousands of troops began the march forward awaiting their opportunity to make that left turn to pass in front of family, high ranking officers, and dignitaries. Doug's moment of glory was at hand. The last column of soldiers in the company before him made their turn, and it was time for him to give orders, "Company, column right." *Right turn? Oh no! That's incorrect,* he said to himself. But it was too late. Although his soldiers realized that their sergeant was in error, they followed in submission to the orders they were given. So, a right turn they made, away from the reviewing stands, off the parade field and down an embankment into a parking lot filled with cars! Doug was so unnerved that in combination with his lack of experience he couldn't remember the correct orders to make his men stop. Meanwhile, his troops continued to march. No longer in perfect columns, they began to mingle among the parked cars. Mercifully, one of the platoon sergeants finally yelled, "Company halt."

There was no doubt from those in attendance who was responsible. Doug was humiliated. However, those closest to him, especially those under his command, realized that he was inexperienced. After all, anyone can make a mistake, and with a little time his blunder would be forgotten. Yet, if you were to hear this story today from Doug's point of view, you would believe that someone else had been responsible for his failure to execute the proper command. Once his soldiers returned to their barracks, it became obvious that Doug was not about to "lose face." Immediately, he began to question their heritage, demean their worth, and affix blame upon *them* for making him look like a fool. His only thought was to soothe his damaged ego by having his men carry the burden of his inexperience and the resulting mistake. Because of this, his days as a drill instructor were numbered. For the sake of pride and humility, he became a leader no longer to be followed.

Doug's mishap on the parade grounds is rather humorous. But imagine what it would have been like to be a member of his family watching in the stands! It has been said that the beginning of wisdom is knowing the fool in us. And like Doug, the overprotected child in a position of leadership is too consumed with himself to honestly consider the reality of this statement in his own life. Those who must live or associate with such a person view him as a king with an oversized crown, holding a scepter too heavy to carry. He has an agenda to fulfill, one that his overprotective past has ordained since the earliest days of his life—to find security in others while satisfying his own desires.

Larry Bryant, one of the finest Christian singers and songwriters today, knows of whom I'm speaking. The lyrics to Larry's song entitled *Shopping List* presents further insight into the personality of the Christian who is a spoiled adult:

Lord I need to talk to you,
There's so much on my heart,
So many burdens makes it hard
To know just where to start.
Thank you for your family,
Your mercy and your love.
Now, on to more important things;
I'll give my magic lamp a rub.

Give me this, I want that,
Bless me Lord I pray,
Grant me what I think I need
To make it through the day.
Make me wealthy, keep me healthy,
Fill in what I missed
On my never-ending shopping list.

Lord you've been so good to me,
How could I ask for more?
But since you said to ask, I will,
Cause what else is prayer for?
The cattle on a thousand hills,
They all belong to you.
I don't need any cows right now,
But something else might do.

Give me this, I want that,
Bless me Lord I pray,
Grant me what I think I need
To make it through the day.
Make me wealthy, keep me healthy,

Fill in what I missed
On my never-ending shopping list.

I've made my list and I checked it twice
If I got it all, it would sure be nice.
I want a nice white smile on a perfect face,
And perfect hair that will stay in place,
I want a smaller nose and a single chin,
And a figure like a perfect ten,
And a mom that never yells or screams,
And hips that fit in designer jeans,
And a tennis court and a heated pool,
I can use them, Lord, as a witnessing tool,
And a color TV, and a VCR,
And Jesus plates on a brand new car.

Give me this, I want that,
Bless me Lord I pray,
Grant me what I think I need
To make it through the day.
Make me wealthy, keep me healthy,
Fill in what I missed
On my never-ending shopping list.[1]

The spoiled adult in leadership may not want the cattle on a thousand hills, a VCR, or Jesus plates on a brand new car, but he has a shopping list nevertheless. He is convinced that if he were only to obtain the items on *his* list that he would experience the self-worth, love, and security for which he has been longing all these years. He has yet to realize, however, that he is only shifting some of his dependency away from those who have overprotected him to more selfish pursuits. Instead of honestly submitting himself to God's authority, he gives his magic lamp a rub. If he were really candid and allowed us to look deeply into his heart, the first wish he would most likely ask for would be, "Give me control."

Actually, this wish would be more accurate if it were to read "Let me continue in my control," for *it is the need to*

© Wayne Stayskal, *Tampa Tribune*, Tampa, Florida.

overcontrol one's environment and those therein that is the hallmark of the spoiled adult's life.

Wayne Stayskal is one of the most successful cartoonists in America today, and his success is characterized by his unique ability to reflect the most serious of issues in a humorous fashion. Perhaps within this cartoon you see reflected within your own family a spoiled "child" in leadership. It accurately depicts how selfish and resentful he becomes of anyone who will not maintain the easy road of life that he has grown accustomed to since he was a child. His unreasonableness should not come as a surprise because, after all, he has been conditioned to believe that his wish is a reasonable expectation for others to meet. It is merely an extension of a line of thinking that has been nurtured and reinforced throughout the years by his overprotective environment. Thus, in his eyes, it is natural that others should march to his own cadence.

Keeping pace along with his need to control others is his second wish which is, "Fill my void of loneliness." Ironically, his second wish stands in direct opposition to his first because loneliness is the end product of an interpersonal relationship based upon a control mentality. The "I'm-the-top-dog—you're-the-underdog" style of leadership may be necessary in directing military personnel, but for the Christian household it can become a battleground all its own.

There is a subtle implication associated with this form of leadership that attacks the worth of the individual who has the least control. This is the assumption that the person exercising the most authority also has more value, or always has greater insight as to how the family ought to function. If this line of thinking is adopted as the norm, eventually it will demoralize the other family members because they will feel controlled and devalued. In light of this, the spoiled adult cannot have it both ways—the need to control and the need for intimacy—because this combination only *creates* feelings of estrangement and loneliness.

Several years ago I spoke with Denise, a middle-aged woman who was married for over twenty years to a man who had been raised in an overprotective household. As a child, Jim received virtually everything his little heart desired and, unfortunately, one of his main reasons for marrying Denise was his belief that she would continue that policy. I asked her to describe in one word what it felt like to have lived with such a man, and her reply was "Trapped!" In her opinion, no matter which way she turned she couldn't please him. In order to submit to his requests, many times she had to violate godly principles.

Loneliness was a daily struggle for both of them, and each tried to fill the void in separate ways. Some of her greatest desires were for Jim to give her a hug . . . a love note on her pillow . . . or to ask her opinion regarding a solution to a difficult problem in his life. But despite his years of marriage, Jim was ill-equipped from childhood to open himself and become vulnerable. To do this would have been very threatening for him, so instead he communicated his worth and love by showing Denise how smart he was, and through his sexuality. But Denise didn't want a hug with hidden expectations or for her husband to prove his intelligence. All she wanted to know was that he needed her, that his life was incomplete without her, and that she was valued by him.

She was more than willing to overlook his awkwardness in expressing his true feelings. In working together, she said, they could fill the void of loneliness. But to entrust her with such a highly vulnerable part of his life would have required Jim to let loose of some of his control—to lower his defenses and give Denise permission to take the lead in helping him to become more open and secure. This, however, was too risky. His need for love and intimacy was overcome by his fear of rejection. As a result, his hardened shell became even more impenetrable, and they continued in their loneliness. The following poem entitled "The Wall" is a beautiful yet tragic depiction of Jim and Denise's relationship:

Their wedding picture mocked them from the table, these two whose minds no longer touched each other.

They lived with such a heavy barricade between them that neither battering ram of words nor artilleries of touch could break it down.

Somewhere, between the oldest child's first tooth and the youngest daughter's graduation, they lost each other.

Throughout the years, each slowly unraveled that tangled ball of string called self, and as they tugged at stubborn knots each hid his searching from the other.

Sometimes she cried at night and begged the whispering darkness to tell her who she was.

He lay beside her, snoring like a hibernating bear, unaware of her winter.

Once, after they had made love, he wanted to tell her how

afraid he was of dying, but, fearing to show his naked soul, he spoke instead about the beauty of her breasts.

She took a course in modern art, trying to find herself in colors splashed upon a canvas, and complaining to other women about men who were insensitive.

He climbed into a tomb called "the office," wrapped his mind in a shroud of paper figures and buried himself in customers.

Slowly, the wall between them rose, cemented by the mortar of indifference.

One day, reaching out to touch each other, they found a barrier they could not penetrate, and recoiling from the coldness of the stone, each retreated from the stranger on the other side.

For when love dies, it is not in a moment of angry battle, nor when fiery bodies lose their heat.

It lies panting, exhausted, expiring at the bottom of a wall it could not scale.[2]

The emotional content of this poem truly reflects the nature of Jim and Denise's marriage. The wall of protection that had been created when Jim was a child to shelter him from emotional discomfort had now become a barrier against intimacy. Jim's emotional restraints held them both captive, causing Denise to seriously contemplate leaving him. But she could not. She felt alone, helpless and trapped—like a caged animal wanting to be free. For Jim, his loneliness prevailed—he was ensnared by his own self-sufficiency. Denise questioned how she could have been so fooled by his lack of emotional maturity. Early into their courtship she remembered that Jim had been this way, but then, as if by magic, he became warm and affectionate. Soon thereafter, they began to develop a common bond with each other. However, barely a week after their wedding, he reverted to his old nature. "How could this be?" she asked.

I mentioned in an earlier chapter that as the spoiled child grows into adulthood, he continues in his search for self-worth. Because of his self-centeredness, he has experienced considerable rejection, and as a result, he adjusts his life-style, attitudes, and mannerisms to reestablish interpersonal relationships. So the spoiled adult has learned how to present a mask of maturity to win friends and influence people. In a sense, he is an emotional con artist who is a picture of emotional health on the outside, but inwardly remains just as insecure as he has always been.

It is because of this that a spoiled adult is usually detected—by watching the types of people he chooses as his friends. With few exceptions, he will also choose as his *mate* a person who has a lower self-esteem than himself and, therefore, one whom he can dominate. This is especially true of men, because a woman with a high degree of self-confidence and worth is threatening to such a man. He cannot control a woman like this because her own level of esteem will not tolerate it. Therefore, the spoiled adult enters into such relationships with his mask of maturity, searching for a mate who he believes is less secure than he, one who will not challenge his selfish authority.

This occurs more often than we might think, and in the case of Jim and Denise's relationship, it was clearly established from the very beginning. As a child, Denise lived within an abusive home. Her father hit her, was very controlling and said very little to cause her to believe in herself. She entered into her adult years with a very low self-esteem, and as a result, one of the ingredients that drew her close to Jim was her need for security. Little did she realize, however, that Jim was feeling the same way. Both insecure, yet for different reasons, each individually rested their hopes for a secure identity on the other.

With this in mind, nothing is more potentially dangerous for a Christian marriage than becoming dependent upon your spouse as the sole source of strength for a positive self-image. In saying this, I am not trying to suggest that a husband or wife is not an integral part of God's plan to restore a bruised or damaged self-concept. However, it is for the reason which I have just stated that many men and women feel trapped within a marriage. If their identity becomes too dependent upon their mate, then perhaps for the sake of not wanting to experience any further rejection or loneliness, they will tolerate, or willingly submit to the desires of their spouse even though what is being asked of them may be unbiblical. In this regard, there is an old saying that goes like this: "If you don't give a child a kiss, he will accept a kick, but he won't accept nothing!" Unfortunately, Denise believed there was something worse than emotional abuse—and that was abandonment.

We can see from this that, for fear of being rejected, deep-seated insecurity within a marriage could be a loaded gun in the hands of a spouse who is a spoiled adult. The low self-esteem and fear of loneliness can be used to coerce obedience out of his or her mate simply to satisfy a selfish need to maintain control. Too often I have seen, under the guise of biblical authority, a husband or wife being asked to submit to that which is obviously outside the will of God.

In my office a short time ago, a mother of two young children came for an appointment to discuss the following question, "How can I learn to be more submissive to my husband?" This can be a question filled with land mines without all the proper details, so I asked her to explain why she was finding it so difficult to follow in her husband's leadership. It has been my experience that when seeking clarification on such a potentially volatile issue, two answers are provided—the *good* one first, followed by the *real* one. Her good answer was an admission that she was very angry, and since she knew it was not God's will, she desired Christian counsel to resolve it. But then, as I began to probe further, the real answer began to emerge.

It was obvious that what she was about to tell me was

very troubling. With head bowed, and in a soft voice, she admitted that one year earlier her husband, in a moment of impulsive anger, pushed her, causing her to trip and fall backwards, hitting her back on the pointed end of the living room coffee table. One would think that once he realized his grave error that he would have come to her aid, but he did not. Instead, as she lay there on the floor injured and in pain, his thoughts were only consumed with himself and how he could "save face." After lecturing her on her clumsiness, he went further and forbade her to talk with anyone or to receive medical attention!

As I continued my conversation with her, it became apparent that her husband's behavior had not stopped here. There were several times which followed his initial outburst where he slapped his wife, and on one occasion he threw her to the floor and began to choke her while sitting on her chest. This, however, was not the utmost reason for her presence in counseling. Despite her husband's abusiveness and total disregard for her worth and integrity, it was not her own welfare that she was concerned with—it was for her son and daughter. Although she had tried her best to disguise her feelings, finally the truth emerged—her husband was abusing them as well. As the parent of two young children, I tried to empathize with her pain. And as she explained in further detail, it was difficult for me to believe that any man, especially one who called himself a Christian, could be so ruthless toward his little ones. During one of his tirades in which he tried to abuse his wife, she decided that she had had enough, threatening that if he were to ever hit her again that she would leave. Her courageous stand, however, was costly. In response to her boldness, he picked up their nine-month-old boy and threw him across the living room. Bouncing off the wall, the infant fell to the floor with a concussion. Again, he threatened his wife to be silent about what he had done. As she reached down to raise her son's limp, unconscious body off the floor, she realized that she could not fully submit to his request. With her injured son draped over one shoulder and her two-year-old daughter in tow, she rushed to the hospital explaining to the emergency room personnel that her son had fallen while climbing on the kitchen table. Fortunately, her son had suffered only a mild concussion and would recover quickly.

Upon hearing this, it would have been ludicrous for me to encourage her to remain within the home and live under her husband's authority. It was no longer a question of submissiveness but rather of her family's survival. For the next few hours after our appointment, I worked in close cooperation with the local authorities and a close relative to provide her family with the love and security they deserved.

What most disturbed me about the events which followed was the response of her husband and her pastor. Together, they stood united in opposition to her desire to separate. Based upon the misapplication of Ephesians 5:24, it was their opinion that as the wife she was to submit to her husband in *all* things. How utterly foolish an interpretation! Was it really their expectation for her to believe that for the sake of submission it is God's plan for a husband or wife to jeopardize not only his or her own life but that of children as well?

As in the case with this young mother, some of us have inherited through marriage an overprotected and spoiled child. Since he or she is now an adult and exerts leadership within the home, what should be our response? Very few people have been willing to challenge the spoiled child's self-centered authority. And as a spouse, do *we* have that right? Will it enhance his or her spiritual growth, and that of their family, to remain passive and enable this person in selfish pursuits? Or do we uncover the mask of maturity, in a spirit of love and gentleness, and be the helpmate which God has intended for us to become? If we can find the courage to choose this latter course of action, we must first confront the critical issue of unconditional love and how it relates to submission.

The heart of the gospel of Jesus Christ is love. It weaves

its way through every book of Scripture. And without it, there is no gospel message. The following passage written by the apostle Paul to the Corinthian church is probably the finest summary on the definition of love throughout all of God's Word:

> Love is patient, love is kind. It does not envy, it does not boast, it is not proud. It is not rude, it is not self-seeking, it is not easily angered, it keeps no record of wrongs. Love does not delight in evil but rejoices with the truth. It always protects, always trusts, always hopes, always perseveres (1 Corinthians 13:4–7, NIV).

In light of this passage of Scripture, the most difficult question before us is this: In striving to love our husbands and wives unconditionally, is God asking us to place ourselves in submission to their leadership when that leadership is in direct opposition to His Word? It would be my opinion that to answer in the affirmative would place our spouse in a position of greater authority than our Lord. Does not unconditional love have in fact one condition— that of submission to God first? *Righteousness does not stand in subservience to marital submission, and submission is not a call by God for us to agree with or become willing participants in someone else's sin—spouse or not.* Jesus would never ask us to violate His Word on the request of a friend, relative, or perhaps even in a weak moment a leader within the church. So, why would He do so on behalf of our mate? He couldn't. It would violate His very nature.

I realize at this moment that I am treading on very dangerous ground. Some could interpret what I have just said as an encouragement to rebel against leadership within the home simply on the basis of a marital disagreement. This, however, would be a far-reaching generalization. Obviously, we will have honest disagreements within marriage over what is God's will, with each partner believing that he or she is biblically correct. Differences of opinion are not at issue here, but rather a leader who wants to embrace love and sin at the same moment.

God gives a husband or wife the right to challenge such a blatant contradiction of His purpose for marriage. In Genesis 2:18–25 we witness God's final and most beautiful creation—woman. Setting other theological arguments aside, it was the Lord's belief that Adam was incomplete and alone with only God at His side. Therefore, He created a "helper" suitable for him. This Hebrew root word for "helper" is *azar* (aw-zar) which means literally to "protect or aid." As evidenced within Ephesians 5:25–30, it is clear that the role of "helper" is not just one dimensional—wife helping husband, but also reciprocal—husband helping wife. However, it was never God's intention that in becoming a helper we were to protect our spouses while they committed sin or to assist (aid) them in doing so. *Biblical love demonstrated within a Christian marriage is not becoming an accomplice in a partner's sinful life-style.*

Thus, to respond passively only allows our home to become a haven of rest for the spoiled adult who stands in rebellion to God's authority. Our lack of assertiveness is viewed as permission to continue, and submitting to such self-centeredness reinforces it to occur again. If we are going to break the spoiled adult's selfishness and preserve our own sense of integrity and self-respect, then we must be willing to follow through with the words of the apostle Paul who said in Galatians 6:1:

> Brethren, if a man (or woman) is overtaken in any trespass, you who are spiritual should restore him in a spirit of gentleness . . . (parentheses mine).

It is our goal, therefore, not to withdraw love, but rather to shed those accouterments of love that serve as a license to perpetuate an endless chain of sinful actions. If a spouse has a drinking problem, we don't buy him alcohol, nor do we contribute a portion of our weekly salary for him to do so. Do we purchase drugs for a drug abuser, or allow him to grow or manufacture it within our home? Should we believe the spouse who is a compulsive gambler when he says, "Today is my lucky day, and all I need, one more time, is another hundred dollars to play the horses, cards, or the "one-armed bandit"? Obviously not. *Love does not contain within its definition contributing to the destruction of those whom we love.*

Our attempts to be tough with our love, however, may be met with a flurry of resistance and criticism. Several years ago I met a young newlywed who had the courage to put into practice the words just spoken by the apostle Paul. She had just celebrated her first wedding anniversary. Yet the tears she shed were not of joy, but rather bewilderment. One evening, upon returning home from work, her husband began to act bizarre. As he walked through the front door she began to greet him as usual, but he rudely pushed her aside. Failing to acknowledge her presence, he then proceeded to pull down the blinds of every window within the house! From bedrooms to bathrooms and on to those rooms which remained, he continued in his ritual. Upon completion of this, he then drew the curtains as well. Still maintaining his silence, he then turned off all the lights, sat in the middle of the living room floor, and began to rock back and forth, in a fetal position, in the gloomy darkness of their home. With his wife emotionally shaken and pleading with him to reveal why he was so disturbed, he finally looked at her, with tears in his eyes, and whispered, "Honey, I am a homosexual. I have always been a homosexual. I love you, but I've got a boyfriend, and I'm not going to give him up." Despite her anguish, her love for him remained, and I was committed along with her to help repair their broken relationship. She became encouraged as he agreed to seek professional advice, yet, although he had confessed a personal relationship with Christ, he would have nothing to do with Christian counseling. Instead, he went to the counseling center of a major university in Southern California. Upon the invitation of his psychiatrist and psychologist, she met together with them privately, whereby, they proceeded for over an hour to harshly criticize her for being intolerant of her husband's lifestyle. "After all," they said, "let him do his own thing; what right do you have for being so judgmental?" With permission like this from two humanistic professionals, her husband found little motivation to change.

To answer their question, the wife had every right to judge her husband's behavior and question his leadership because she had the authority of Scripture behind her. No, the Lord had not given her the privilege to judge his relationship with God; however, neither did He want her wedding vows to be used as an invitation to court evil. If it meant that she had to separate from her husband and seek Christian counseling in order to communicate the gravity of his rebelliousness, then it was worth loving him that much in order to salvage their marriage.

In light of this newlywed's predicament, the Christian church many times stands as a miserable failure. While we stand in the pulpits and preach against separation and divorce, we neglect to help those who have biblically legitimate reasons to do so. As a result, the church perpetuates a cycle of dependency by those spouses and their children whose husband or wife abuses a position of authority within the home. What do we expect them to do? If the church is unwilling to provide financial assistance, food, and temporary housing, then do we abandon them to other alternatives—perhaps to live on the streets? The church needs to be reminded of the sensitivity expressed by our Lord Jesus when he said in Matthew 25:34–40:

Then the King will say to those at his right hand, "Come, O blessed of my Father, inherit the kingdom prepared for you from the foundation of the world; for I was hungry and you gave me food, I was thirsty and you gave me drink, I was a stranger and you welcomed me, I was naked and you clothed me, I was sick and you visited me, I was in prison and you came to me." Then the righteous will answer him, "Lord when did we see thee hungry and feed thee, or thirsty and gave thee drink? And when did we see thee a stranger and welcome thee, or naked and clothe thee? And when did we see thee sick or in prison and visit thee?" And the King will answer them, "Truly, I say to you, as you did it to one of the least of these my brethren, you did it to me."

As I was writing this book, one of my secretaries approached me to ask who was significantly involved in helping me change from my early years of insecurity and selfishness. I could devote pages in thanking those who have been instrumental in transforming my life, however, without a doubt, the greatest thank you needs to be extended toward my wife, Diane. Despite her outward beauty and intelligence, which drew me to her originally, I will be eternally grateful for her inner beauty and refusal to believe that I was impossible to live with or a hopeless case. Her love and devotion has not extended itself to such a degree that she has failed to hold me accountable when I have been wrong. Neither has she rescued me from my bouts with irresponsibility, though she could have spared me some pain had she done so. Furthermore, and most importantly, she has spoken the truth in love even to the point of challenging my authority.

The trophies in Christian leadership will not be awarded to the men and women who have the greatest success in forcing others to submit to their leadership, but rather, to those men and women like my wife who, by modeling love, cause others to cease in their own self-direction and submit to the Lord's direction instead. Hopefully, my two daughters will acknowledge this beauty within their mother. If it hadn't been for her, my little girls would have had a father who embodied the words inscribed upon the license plate holder setting on a car parked in front of my home one day, which said, "I may be getting older, but I refuse to grow up!"

Thank you for allowing me to share my convictions with you. My heartfelt prayer is that this book can be one more tool in helping you become equipped to raise your children in the love and admonition of Jesus Christ, children you (and the world) can live with!

---

[1] Written by Larry Bryant and Lesa Bryant. Copyright 1984 Meadowgreen Music Co., All rights Adm. by Tree Pub. Co. Inc. 8 Music Sq.W. Nashville, Tenn. Int'l Copyright secured, All rights reserved, Used by permission.
[2] Author Unknown

APPENDIX

Authoritarian: (High control, not much support)
1, 2, 6, 17, 18

Neglectful: (Little or no control, little or no support)
5, 7, 8, 10, 14

Permissive: (Child senses he is in the driver's seat)
4, 12, 13, 16, 20

Authoritative: (A tone of control, tempered with a feeling
of support)
3, 9, 11, 15, 19

Taken from *What Kind of Parent Are You?* By Dennis Guernsey in Family Life Today, January 1975. Used by permission of Dr. Guernsey. Copyright by Gospel Light Publications, Glendale, California 91204.